Europe: One Continent, Different Worlds: Population Scenarios for the 21st Century

European Studies of Population

VOLUME 7

The book series *European Studies of Population (ESPO)* aims at disseminating population and family research, with special relevance for Europe. It may analyse past, present and/or future trends, as well as their determinants and consequences.

The character of the series is multidisciplinary, including formal demographic analyses, as well as social, economic and/or historical population and family studies.

The following types of studies are of primary importance: (a) internationally relevant studies, (b) European comparative studies, (c) innovative theoretical and methodological studies, and (d) policy-relevant scientific studies. The series may include monographs, edited volumes and reference works.

The book series is published under the auspices of the *European Association for Population Studies (EAPS)*.

Europe: One Continent, Different Worlds

Population Scenarios for the 21st Century

edited by

JOOP DE BEER and LEO VAN WISSEN

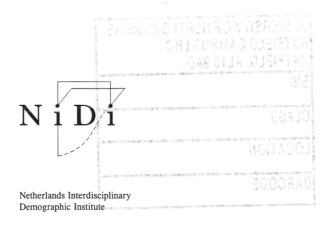

NiDi

Netherlands Interdisciplinary
Demographic Institute

Statistics Netherlands

KLUWER ACADEMIC PUBLISHERS
DORDRECHT / BOSTON / LONDON

A C.I.P. Catalogue record for this book is available from the Library of Congress.

ISBN 0-7923-5840-6 (HB)

Published by Kluwer Academic Publishers,
P.O. Box 17, 3300 AA Dordrecht, The Netherlands.

Sold and distributed in North, Central and South America
by Kluwer Academic Publishers,
101 Philip Drive, Norwell, MA 02061, U.S.A.

In all other countries, sold and distributed
by Kluwer Academic Publishers,
P.O. Box 322, 3300 AH Dordrecht, The Netherlands.

Printed on acid-free paper

Printed in the Netherlands.

Table of Contents

viii

Preface

On the threshold of a new century the organisers of the European Population Conference 1999 (EPC99) in The Hague decided not only to highlight the population trends that Europe is facing today but also the changes in the 21st century that are set to shape the future of Europe. They decided to focus on comparative issues, both in time and in space. In order to trace the degree of homogeneity and heterogeneity of European populations over time, converging and diverging population trends that are specific to contemporary and future Europe need to be explored. This is reflected in EPC99's motto: 'European Populations on the threshold of the new millennium; unity in diversity.'

Future demographic developments will be caused by specific economic, social and cultural conditions in Europe, and will, in turn, have a major influence on future economic and social conditions. To the extent that demographic trends differ across countries, separate countries may face different social and economic problems. As demographic trends tend to have long-lasting effects, it is important to assess the possible consequences of future demographic developments at an early stage. On the occasion of EPC99, two of the organisers, Statistics Netherlands (SN) and the Netherlands Interdisciplinary Demographic Institute (NIDI), decided to produce a set of two population scenarios, showing the possible impact of converging and diverging population trends in the next century.

Europe is an interesting continent for social scientists as it has experienced many crucial events over the past decades (e.g. the creation of the European Union and the transition of central and eastern European societies from communism to a market system) that may alter future demographic patterns. Large cultural and economic variations exist, but there is also a growing tendency among European countries to co-operate and integrate. Moreover, demographic developments in many European countries are strikingly similar (see e.g. Harding *et al.*, 1986; Kuijsten, 1996). This raises the question whether convergent or divergent trends will dominate long-term future demographic developments in the countries of Europe. Since there is no unambiguous answer to this question, this book describes two alternative scenarios for Europe's future population.

In the Uniformity scenario, convergent forces are dominant. This will eventually lead to a situation where only marginal economic and cultural differences exist across Europe. Trends in fertility and mortality will converge up to the year 2050, although over-time patterns may differ across countries as a result of their different initial states. Since this scenario assumes that Europe will be economically and culturally homogeneous in the long run, other factors that influence migration become important. Individuals choose to live in the country they prefer and are not bound by their country of birth. In contrast to the Uniformity scenario, a Diversity scenario is constructed where cultural, economic and demographic characteristics remain significantly different across countries.

On the basis of the two sets of assumptions about future fertility, mortality and migration, the population scenarios project changes in the size and age structure of the population over the next 50 years for 33 European countries. This book describes the specific assumptions underlying the scenarios and presents the main demographic outcomes. The enclosed CD-ROM with the *Scenariobrowser* includes detailed results.

This book is largely the result of close collaboration between a number of researchers from SN and NIDI. In order to fully reflect the joint character of this endeavour, it would have been necessary to include a long list of authors on the cover of the book. Since this was not feasible, the form of an edited volume was chosen with separate chapters by small groups of authors. The authors are indeed responsible for writing their contribution, but they were also often involved to a certain extent in the realisation of some of the other chapters as well.

The editors gratefully acknowledge the very useful comments on a previous version of the scenarios by David Coleman, Stephane Cotter, Harri Cruijsen, Virginija Eidukiene, Alexander Hanika, Gert Hullen, Dirk Van de Kaa, Nico Keilman, Jean Langers, Luc Lebrun, Miroslav Macura, Grazyna Marciniak, Annie Mesrine, Robin Rich, Chris Shaw, Maria Pia Sorvillo, Michal Tirpak, Boris Vano, and Peteris Zvidrins. Their input has given this project a truly

European dimension. Moreover, the editors owe thanks to many people who contributed in various ways in the course of the project. Erik Beekink, from the NIDI, was responsible for the database EDAT, on which the scenarios are based. Willemien Kneppelhout and Anne Marksman did a thorough job in checking the English language, and Joan Vrind (NIDI) was responsible for the technical editing and layout of the manuscript, which she did within a tight time schedule but with great care. Having said that, the authors remain responsible for the contents of their contributions, and the editors for any remaining errors in the book.

Prof. Dr. J.Gierveld
Director,
Netherlands Interdisciplinary
Demographic Institute

Prof. Dr. A.P.J. Abrahamse
Director-General,
Statistics Netherlands

List of Authors

Joop DE BEER	Statistics Netherlands
Rob BROEKMAN	Statistics Netherlands
Nicole VAN DER GAAG	Netherlands Interdisciplinary Demographic Institute
Wim VAN HOORN	Statistics Netherlands
Corina HUISMAN	Netherlands Interdisciplinary Demographic Institute
Evert VAN IMHOFF	Netherlands Interdisciplinary Demographic Institute
Andries DE JONG	Statistics Netherlands
Martin MELLENS	Statistics Netherlands
Leo VAN WISSEN	Netherlands Interdisciplinary Demographic Institute

Statistics Netherlands, P.O. Box 4000, 2270 JM Voorburg
Netherlands Interdisciplinary Demographic Institute, P.O. Box 11650,
2502 AR The Hague

List of Figures

List of Tables

1. Introduction to the Uniformity and Diversity Scenarios

Joop DE BEER and Leo VAN WISSEN

Future demographic developments will have a major influence on economic and social conditions in Europe. Ageing, for example, affects consumption patterns, the demand for health care, pension schemes and labour supply. Population growth has an impact on the physical environment and the housing market while an increase in the population of foreign descent has far-reaching social consequences. As demographic trends tend to have long-term effects, it is important that we assess the possible consequences of future developments at an early stage. For assessments of this sort, we need population scenarios for the long term. In view of the uncertainties inherent in forecasts for the long term, it is useful to take into account possible divergent developments by specifying alternative scenarios rather than a single forecast. Scenarios describe feasible future trends while acknowledging that the future is inherently unpredictable. In a scenario we create a possible future image of society, based on cause and effect relationships within a model of society. It is therefore a potentially useful instrument for reflecting on the future.

This book presents two population scenarios for the first half of the 21st century for 33 European countries. The study differs from projections in the field of demography in that the scenarios are not based on an extrapolation of the components of population growth, but are rooted in assumptions about the economic and cultural developments in a country. In

1

J. de Beer and L. van Wissen (eds.),
European: One Continent, Different Worlds Population Scenarios for the 21st Century, 1–4.
© 1999 Kluwer Academic Publishers. Printed in the Netherlands.

this way, the scenarios are based explicitly on hypotheses with respect to future developments in the cultural and socioeconomic determinants of demographic behaviour.

More specifically, one of the basic assumptions underlying the scenarios is that developments in fertility, mortality and migration depend on economic and cultural changes. Some trends are similar in most European countries, even though the timing and intensity of the trends may differ. For example, in most European countries economic structures have changed, the role of religion has declined and the status of women has improved. Accordingly, most countries have witnessed similar demographic trends: the level of fertility has declined strongly since the beginning of the century, life expectancy at birth has risen, and the number of international migrants has increased. Nevertheless there are still significant differences between countries in Europe. One obvious example is the difference in standards of living between the former communist states and western Europe. But there are also economic differences between northern and southern countries. Economic structures, for example, differ across countries and there are considerable institutional differences, e.g. with respect to flexibility in the labour market and social security. In addition, large cultural differences exist regarding, among other things, the importance of family values, individual responsibility, the emancipation of women and materialism. These economic and cultural differences go hand in hand with important demographic differences. For example, fertility is high in northern Europe and low in southern Europe; life expectancy is high in northern and southern Europe and low in eastern Europe.

One major source of uncertainty regarding demographic trends in the 21st century is the question whether the differences between countries will decline as a result of common economic and cultural trends, or whether the differences will persist or even increase. In view of this uncertainty two scenarios have been compiled.

The Uniformity scenario assumes that in the long run economic and cultural trends will converge and consequently differences across countries will decline. Economic structures are set to change in all countries, induced by increased automation and technology. In addition, living standards will rise, and emancipation and individualisation are expected to forge ahead.

Differences in fertility, mortality and migration rates will thus become smaller.

The Diversity scenario, on the other hand, assumes that both economic and cultural differences between countries will persist or even increase. The degree of market orientation, economic structures and standards of living will differ significantly between countries. There will be a convergence of superficial aspects of culture due to the influence of the mass media, but not of more fundamental values, such as individualism, materialism, assertiveness, family values, et cetera. In this scenario, the levels of fertility, mortality and migration will remain different in northern, western, southern, and central and eastern European countries. The scenarios explore the impact of these alternative assumptions on changes in the size and age structure of the population of 33 European countries in the first half of the 21st century.

The explanatory approach followed in this study focuses on the determinants of a particular development, rather than estimating a single, most accurate prediction on the basis of extrapolation. The explanatory approach may be more useful in finding stable segments and long-term patterns, especially under heavily fluctuating circumstances (Day et al., 1979; Quellette and Wood, 1998). Moreover, it offers the possibility of basing the scenarios on demographic theory and enables researchers to state explicitly the cultural/economic assumptions underlying the scenarios. A drawback of the approach is that the link between the explanatory variables and the scenarios is imperfect by definition, as it is impossible to include all the variables that influence population dynamics. Given the large number of variables involved and the complex relationship between the variables, the empirical evidence of a particular variable's impact may be either weak or ambiguous.

A different approach to exploring future demographic developments is the extrapolation of demographic components by time-series techniques. A disadvantage of this approach is that only over-time fluctuations of fertility, life expectancy and migration are studied and not their causes. We are therefore unable to find out whether observed similar patterns between countries are purely co-incidental, whether they are the result of similar changes in determining variables or whether they are due to the fact that two countries are at a similar stage in their demographic development. A related issue is that past behaviour may not be an accurate predictor of future behaviour since circumstances may change. The extrapolation approach may therefore provide fairly accurate predictions for the short term, but its predictive validity for the long term is questionable. Indeed, the longer the time span under consideration, the greater the probability that the situation will change. This is an important issue in this study since it includes central and eastern European countries, which have experienced a structural break in their economic and cultural climate. In view of these disadvantages, the extrapolation approach is less suitable for the purposes of this study. We have therefore opted for the explanatory scenario approach.

Based on these considerations, this book describes the construction of two scenarios of population trends in European countries for the first half of the 21st century. The demographic processes are determined by two basic dimensions: a socioeconomic dimension and a cultural dimension. In Chapter 2, the relationships between these two dimensions and demographic dynamics are established. Data have been collected for a large number of characteristics of many European countries and these data are analysed to validate the theoretical construction base of the scenarios. Although this serves to assess the validity of our approach, it is not our main purpose to construct a complete explanatory model.

An important element of the scenario approach, presented in Chapter 3, is the clustering of European countries into five homogeneous groups, based on their socioeconomic and cultural dimensions. This clustering of countries, rather than working with 33 individual countries, is necessary to keep the discussion manageable and transparent. The theoretical and empirical analysis provides a framework for a qualitative discussion to assess benchmarks for the economic and cultural developments observed in the European countries studied. The benchmarks are used to construct the assumed patterns of fertility, life expectancy and migration for the two scenarios, which are discussed in detail in Chapters 4, 5 and 6, respectively. The main outcomes of the two scenarios are presented in Chapter 7. A separate CD-ROM containing more detailed results is provided as an annex to this book. Appendix 2 gives a short introduction to the *Scenario Browser* programme on the CD-ROM. Chapter 8 discusses a number of possible implications of the scenarios and summarises the main conclusions.

2. Determinants of Demographic Behaviour

Martin MELLENS

2.1 | Theoretical Framework

A survey of the academic literature in the field of demography reveals a large number of variables that may influence population dynamics. To keep the discussion manageable, we have to classify these variables into several groups, which may be regarded as the underlying dimensions of the population patterns. In this study, we distinguish two broad dimensions, one of them may reflect the tangible (physical) features of a country while the other describes the intangible characteristics, which may reflect the 'image' of a country. The first factor is labelled the *socioeconomic dimension* as it is strongly related to the socioeconomic variables that determine a country's current and future economic wealth and refers to its economic, physical and human-capital characteristics. The other is labelled the *cultural dimension* as it refers to the values that are important for a particular society and which are in line with a nation's culture. Although different categorisations might be used (see e.g. Matutinovic (1998) for an example of an alternative division), these dimensions are in line with those mentioned by many demographic researchers (see e.g. Lesthaeghe and Surkyn, 1988).

It may be argued that the actions of policy-makers form a separate third dimension. They may encourage individual behaviour by incentives (e.g. tax systems that favour married couples) or influence behaviour through legislation (e.g. migration laws). Indeed, in some countries policy-makers

5

J. de Beer and L. van Wissen (eds.),
European: One Continent, Different Worlds Population Scenarios for the 21st Century, 5–32.
© 1999 Kluwer Academic Publishers. Printed in the Netherlands.

have tried to stimulate or discourage demographic behaviour by policy actions (Beaujot, 1991; Höhn, 1991a; Jozan, 1991). Having said that, we shall not treat politics as a separate element. In order to be effective, a policy needs to be rooted in the cultural value system of the population and should be in line with economic processes. Particular choices made by politicians may reflect the cultural values of a society and may therefore be regarded as an outcome of culture rather than a separate element. Economic performance may also be the result of political actions as a sound legal framework is a necessary condition for an efficient market. These issues show that it may be difficult to separate the political component from the socioeconomic and cultural components. We therefore assume that politics is captured adequately by the socioeconomic and cultural dimensions, and that it is not necessary to model it as a separate factor. However, since cultural and economic developments may have political implications and vice versa, political aspects are mentioned when the scenarios are applied.

Lifestyle may also have a substantial impact on a country's population dynamics. For example, a reduction in the proportion of smokers has increased life expectancy. The lifestyle of an individual depends on his or her personality and socioeconomic background, and on the social rules of a particular society. To illustrate the importance of the last element, an individual may have sexually promiscuous intentions but may restrict behaviour as a result of conservative social morals. The personality element of lifestyle itself is also strongly correlated with the cultural and socioeconomic characteristics of individuals. The variation that is not explained by these factors may be attributed to a biological antecedent or to an individual's personal history. These variables are assumed to be randomly distributed across nations. Hence, only those lifestyle elements that are determined by a nation's cultural and socioeconomic characteristics are important when we evaluate the different population scenarios across countries and there is no need in this study to distinguish separate lifestyle variables.

To assess the theoretical link between the socioeconomic and cultural dimensions on the one hand and fertility, life expectancy and migration on the other we first have to define them more precisely and discuss the nature of their relationships with respect to demographic developments. These issues are complicated by the fact that the two factors are not independent constructs, but may interact with each other. Some researchers argue, for example, that cultural values may be important factors affecting economic growth (e.g. Hofstede and Bond, 1988). Economic developments may, in turn, influence the values considered important by society. For example, if income levels rise, direct material needs may be satisfied and values that emphasise the quality of life may become more important. Another issue is that economic prosperity may be a necessary condition for some cultural developments. A high level of individualism may not be possible in a poor country. A final point is that the socioeconomic and cultural variables do not only cause changes in the components of demographic behaviour, but are in turn influenced by them. For example, shortages of labour in the labour market may be a pull factor for migration. These immigrants enter the labour market, putting downward pressures on wages and thus influencing average income. Since feedback mechanisms between migration on the one hand and the socioeconomic and cultural dimensions on the other hand is rather important, to some extent they have been incorporated in the construction of the scenarios.

The conceptual model underlying the relationships used to construct the scenarios is described in *Figure 2.1*. The variables are marked by squares if they are observable and by ellipses if they are not observable. The solid lines indicate the relationships that have been included in the construction of the scenarios. It is assumed that socioeconomic and cultural factors affect fertility, life expectancy, and migration, which in turn influence population size and age structure. Furthermore, it is assumed that migration affects both the socioeconomic and the cultural environment. The indigenous population may adopt some cultural values or habits from the immigrants, or they may become more ethnocentric or conservative. The feedback included may induce a multiplier effect. For example, a large number of immigrants from a particular country increases the probability that people from the same country will follow. Algerians tend to migrate to France while Moroccans tend to migrate to countries like Belgium and France. This example shows that travelling distance is not the only important factor influencing migration, and that cultural similarity, or the existence of a large minority group of culturally similar individuals, should also be incorporated in migration models. In addition, there may be yet another feedback mechanism, as changes in population size and age structure affect the economic and cultural environment, which in turn affect fertility, mortality and migration. These 'second-order' effects have partly

Figure 2.1. Conceptual model underlying the scenarios

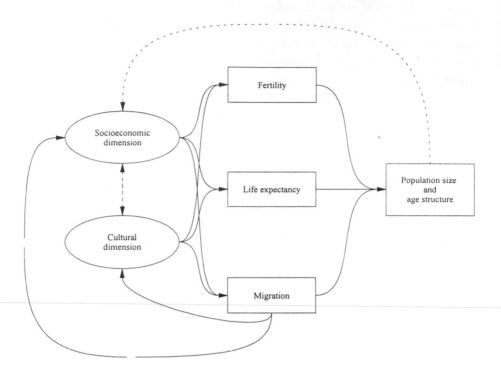

been included in the construction of the scenarios, in particular in the migration component. We will come back to this issue in Chapter 8.

2.2 | The Socioeconomic Dimension

The socioeconomic dimension may be divided into economic, education, health and technology components. In addition to these elements, which may change within a relatively short time span, there are characteristics of a country that are fixed. These fixed variables, such as geographical or climatic characteristics, may also influence life expectancy and fertility in a country, or migration to and from that country. They may be captured by a country-specific factor that reflects the intrinsic nature of that country with respect to population dynamics. However, such a constant may capture the effect of any variable that is not explicitly included in the model and its interpretation may therefore be ambiguous. For that reason, the fixed country-specific characteristics are omitted in the discussion of this chapter.

2.2.1. *Economy*

Several indicators such as the Gross National Product (GNP), the rate of inflation, or the unemployment rate may describe a nation's state of the economy. In most demographic studies, attention is focussed on the relationship between per capita GNP and population dynamics as this factor may be regarded as the most important determinant of this dimension with respect to the three components of demographic change. Per capita GNP may be defined as the average income of a country's inhabitants and it measures the wealth of a nation directly in economic terms.

If we assess the per capita GNP, we see large differences across Europe. Since the Second World War, GNP has increased almost every year for most countries in the EU. After a rapid increase in the 1950s and 1960s, annual growth slowed down in the EU region during the 1970s, turning into an overall recession after the second oil crisis in 1979. Although the European economies recovered during the 1980s, the fluctuations in economic growth were rather large and global performance was relatively weak, in particular compared with the United States. The over-time pattern of the GNP in the Mediterranean countries differs from that in the other members of the EU. Portugal and Greece perform relatively modestly in economic terms while a substantial difference can be observed between the wealthy north and the poor south of Italy, which lowers the national economic output. Spain has developed well economically since its accession to the EU in 1985, but it experienced a major crisis in 1992. Ever since the implementation of the Marshall Plan by the United States in 1948, Europe's democratic governments have economically outperformed the communist states in central and eastern Europe. The differences between these regions have become even more pronounced since the fall of communism. These countries experienced a sharp decline in average income during the transition period (Illner, 1998; Matutinovic, 1998; Zvidrins, 1998). We further see a distinction between those countries that were already rather liberal during the communist era, such as Poland, Hungary and the Czech Republic, and the orthodox communist countries. Now, in the second half of the 1990s, the first group of countries seems to be recovering while the economic recession continues to hold sway in the second group.

Empirical and theoretical studies of the relationship between average income and demographic developments yield ambiguous results (see e.g. Van Hoorn and De Beer, 1998), which may be due to substantial interactions. There may be a negative relationship between the TFR and the GNP, as it increases the opportunity costs of leaving the labour market for women (Becker, 1993). Some researchers also argue that for women a high income reduces the attractiveness of marriage, but the empirical support for this hypothesis is weak (Smock and Manning, 1997). A higher income may also encourage a more individual lifestyle. As having a single household is relatively more expensive than living in a family, a higher prosperity level implies that more people can afford to live individually. Moreover, a high GNP implies that more money is available at a national level to improve the situation on the housing market, which may influence the decision of young people to leave the parental home (Jones, 1995).

Maslow's hierarchy of needs may point to a positive relationship between the TFR and GNP. A higher income means that basic needs (for food, for economic security) are likely to be satisfied and that higher-order motives (e.g. self-actualisation, self expression) become more important. This reasoning is in line with the transition from material to post-material values in recent decades, as stated by Inglehart (1990). Children may be an important element in the satisfaction of such needs. A high income may therefore lead to an increasing TFR, despite the rising opportunity costs of children, because individuals are increasingly prepared to bear the costs of having children. A higher income may also lead to growing confidence in the future, and this may stimulate fertility. This implies that there is a positive relationship between fertility and the consumer confidence index (Van Giersbergen and De Beer, 1997). This reasoning is in line with Easterlin's (1969, 1975, 1976) hypothesis, which states that cohorts with favourable economic perspectives have a higher level of fertility.

The relationship between mortality and GNP is also rather complex. A higher GNP is likely to improve a nation's hygienic conditions and its health care system. Moreover, it may imply that firms have more money to improve working conditions and it may cause a shift from the production of industrial goods to services. A higher income also means that people's diets show more variation, which has positive health implications. Moreover, individuals can afford better medical aid and show lower levels of socio-economic distress. Finally, a higher income is positively correlated with satisfaction in life (Schyns, 1998). For all these reasons, a positive relationship between life expectancy and GNP may be assumed. However, inhabitants of Mediterranean countries live longer despite their lower incomes, which shows that income is not related to life expectancy in a straightforward linear way (Van Hoorn and De Beer, 1998). Growth in GNP may be obtained at the expense of the environment and environmental pollution may decrease life expectancy in the long run. A high income may also imply that the productivity of labour needs to be high, which may induce higher levels of stress, resulting in a lower life expectancy.

The GNP is positively related to net migration as increasing wealth attracts individuals of poorer countries (see e.g. Wils, 1991). A booming economy may also lead to shortages in the labour market, which encourages firms to look for workers abroad. Such a situation occurred in western Europe in the 1960s and is taking place today in some industries in these countries. Moreover, inhabitants of wealthy countries have little incentive to emigrate. Empirical studies confirm the positive relationship between GNP and net migration (see e.g. De Jong and Visser, 1997).

Though many demographic studies focus on income when they study the determinants of demographic behaviour, the level of unemployment may also be an important factor. Individuals who are structurally unemployed are less wealthy and have fewer social contacts. We may therefore assume a negative relationship between the unemployment rate and life expectancy. A high level of unemployment may also cause a reduction in female labour supply. After all, if the opportunities of finding a job are low, women have little incentive to participate in the labour force, and consequently, female labour supply will be lower. This may have a positive influence on the TFR. The most straightforward relationship may be found between unemployment and migration. A low unemployment rate may indicate that firms have difficulty finding workers, which may be a strong pull factor for immigration. Moreover, migrants may choose a particular country if the probability of finding a job there is high.

2.2.2. Education

The level of educational attainment of the population in a country may be seen as an indicator of human capital, which may lead to a higher productivity of labour in the future. According to economic theory, higher productivity leads to higher income and hence education may be seen as an investment designed to obtain a higher income level in the future. The level of education is strongly correlated with GNP for at least two reasons. Firstly, a high GNP implies that more money is available for education. Secondly, a high income means that a higher productivity is needed, which often requires a higher level of education. Therefore, differences in the quality of the education system usually reflect variations in economic wealth. In addition, different nations may organise their education system differently, which may have an impact on the effectiveness of the system. Given these issues, it is not surprising that differences in the level of education and the performance of scholars are observed across European countries (OECD, 1996). However, the level of education is rising in most European countries, in particular the educational attainment of women.

The level of education influences demographic developments in a number of ways. Individuals who pursue an education for a prolonged period of time tend to postpone marriage. As a result, highly educated women tend to have their first child at an older age (Alders and Manting, 1998). Moreover, highly educated women have a better position in the labour market, which may make it harder for them to combine children with a job. As the nurturing of children is still primarily the responsibility of women, they may have to work part-time if they want to have children and this may be harder to achieve if they have a managerial job. The Human Capital theory (Becker, 1975; Mincer and Polachek, 1974) explains the relationship between the female level of education and fertility. Highly educated women tend to have built up considerable human capital and they often want to increase this further by obtaining work experience. However, the realisation of a high income by pursuing a professional career will lead to the postponement of motherhood and increase the risk of involuntary childlessness due to reduced fecundity at older ages. When highly educated women do have children, they often have a smaller number than lower educated women since their first child is often born at an older age. If the distribution of contraceptives is not nationwide, the use of contraceptives may also be positively correlated with education (Kohler, 1997). Better educated people are also less inclined to embrace traditionalism and social conformism, which implies that they are more prone to alternative life-styles (Lesthaeghe and Surkyn, 1988). This may be due to the fact that they have better access to information, and process it more efficiently (Assael, 1992), which increases their awareness of non-traditional lifestyles.

Their access to information also provides them with more extensive knowledge of the potentially negative consequences of their lifestyles. The healthier lifestyles of more highly educated people, as shown in empirical studies, may reflect these differences in access to information. The impact of a healthy lifestyle is further increased by the fact that individuals with a high level of education tend to work under healthier conditions and live in better houses. For all these reasons, we may expect a negative relationship between education and fertility and a positive relationship between education and life expectancy. The importance of education as a determinant of the level of fertility has been shown in an analysis of total fertility rates since 1960 in the Netherlands (De Jong, 1997; Veenhoven, 1996). The hypothesis that having a high income might increase the probability of staying childless was confirmed (De Man and De Jong, 1997). As the educational level is also positively correlated with a person's mobility, highly skilled individuals are more likely to migrate (SOPEMI, 1997). Individuals with a high level of education often have a higher income so they can afford to move to other countries. Moreover, they may also have better insight into job opportunities in other countries. However, the immigration rate is also likely to increase, in particular since if all individuals are better educated, shortages in the lower segments of the labour market may occur. It is therefore difficult to assess the separate effect of education on the migration rate, since its direction and strength may depend heavily on situation-specific characteristics.

2.2.3. Health

The health dimension reflects both the likelihood of becoming ill and the possibility of being cured from illness. Health may reflect an element of wealth, though it may be difficult to measure it directly in terms of money. A healthy individual is often more productive than an unhealthy one and is therefore more likely to earn a higher income. It should be noted that the causal relationship between income and health might be reversed. In times of economic stress, unhealthy lifestyles such as alcohol abuse become more widespread among males. The determinants of the health factor may be divided into individual lifestyles and a social element, which refers to the characteristics of a society that determine the state of health. It may be argued that lifestyle factors are an element of the cultural dimension. In this study, however, they are treated as an element of the socioeconomic dimension, as an unhealthy lifestyle is bound to have repercussions for future labour productivity, and hence the future average income of a country. As such, individuals with healthy lifestyles are a potential asset to a country. An unhealthy lifestyle such as alcohol abuse, smoking or unhealthy dietary habits may have a substantial impact on life expectancy (see e.g. Dinkel, 1985; Van Hoorn, 1993). Estimates in the United States have pointed out that half the difference between male and female life expectancy was due to the higher proportion of smokers among men. The social element includes, among other things, the quality of living and working conditions. Living conditions are determined by a number of factors such as the level of environmental pollution, the housing quality and hygienic conditions. The likelihood of being cured depends primarily on the quality of medical aid.

The quality of a country's medical system, like that of a nation's education system, is strongly correlated with the funds that are available for health care. We observe substantial differences in the health dimension across Europe today (ECE, 1997). On average, the quality of health care in northern and western Europe is better than that in southern, central and eastern Europe. Although the countries of eastern Europe had a fairly well-developed medical system in the communist era, they were more successful in achieving an adequate level of basic health care than in the treatment of more complex diseases such as cancer (Guo, 1993). After the fall of communism, their health care systems were dismantled to cut government expenditures. As a result, substantial proportions of people lack adequate health care. Health care in the Mediterranean countries seems to operate on a smaller scale than in the western European and Scandinavian countries. Data provided by the World Health Organisation (1998) show that less money is spent on health care but that there are relatively more doctors, dentists and nurses. These figures may indicate that medical staff are less educated. The environment component of the health dimension shows a more complex picture. The economically advanced states of Europe pro-duce more waste, as people with a higher income usually demand more products. However, they also have more money to spend on more expensive but cleaner production processes. Moreover, pressure groups seem to have a greater impact in these regions since most of these countries are democracies. For this reason, and since the former communist governments used to emphasise industrial production rather than services, even today environmental pollution is a more acute problem in the former communist countries. The health elements mentioned in the previous paragraph are all related to a greater or lesser degree to the economic development of individual countries. Quite a different element is the individual personality factor. It is rather difficult to categorise the countries of Europe on the basis of this factor, since different personality traits may have different consequences for health and may lead to different clustering. Alcohol abuse seems to be an issue in the countries of eastern Europe and to a lesser extent in the Nordic countries. Data also show that heart diseases are a relatively unimportant cause of death in Mediterranean countries, which might be caused by their healthier diet.

A positive score on the health dimension is naturally positively related to life expectancy. The better the living conditions and the better the medical aid, the higher the probability of surviving to an older age. It is uncertain, however, which element contributes most. Empirical research seems to show that the increase in life expectancy during the last century was not caused primarily by improvements in medical technology, but by improvements in hygiene and nutrition (McKeown, 1976). Still, other research shows that differences in the quality and organisation of the health care system may account for cross-national differences in life expectancy (Guo, 1993). There may also be differences with respect to the time span within which the different elements of health affect life expectancy. Improvements in the health care system offer the opportunity of increasing life expectancy within a relatively short period of time. In contrast, changes in living conditions may only be apparent after a relatively long period of time, in particular if they are modest and the basic requirements are met, as is the case for the majority of European countries.

2.2.4. The State of Technology

Technological improvements may have a direct and an indirect influence on population dynamics. Some researchers argue that the introduction of the contraceptive pill, a technological improvement, was a necessary condition for the second demographic transition (Van de Kaa, 1987, 1994), which was characterised by increasing individualism, increasing female emancipation, and a decreasing fertility rate. Technological medical innovations may also increase life expectancy, but the effect of such improvements is debatable, as mentioned in the previous section. However, technological breakthroughs in the field of genetics may, in the future, help reduce the number of deaths caused by cancer. Technology may also lead to cleaner and more efficient production processes, which may reduce environmental pollution. Finally, the state of technology may have an important indirect impact as it enhances labour productivity. A high productivity of labour leads to a high income, and this in turn may increase life expectancy.

As a result of the introduction of new medical techniques such as in vitro fertilisation, we may also assume that there is a positive relationship between technology and fertility. These techniques may reduce the proportion of women who are unable to have children due to infecundity, and this leads to a higher TFR. However, in empirical settings, this relationship may be hard to find as the number of couples that benefit from these innovations is rather small and because these techniques are not always effective. In addition, other trends such as the fact that women today are bearing their first child at an older age, may offset the positive influence of new techniques. For these reasons, we may assume that the effect of technological developments on fertility is relatively small. It may be conjectured that there is also a positive connection between the state of technology and migration. A more advanced technology makes travelling easier and decreases the relative travelling costs and therefore lowers the perceived distances. Moreover, innovations in global communication systems, such as communication satellites, have increased the global awareness of individuals. An innovation like the Internet allows individuals to communicate directly with individuals of other cultures. All these facilities provide access to information from a large variety of countries and cultures. For these reasons, we may assume that cultural and economic barriers for migration will be smaller. Having said that, it is hard to postulate whether the migration balance is positive or negative, since the reasons mentioned decrease the costs for both immigrants and emigrants. We may thus assume that technological developments act as a catalyst for migration, but that the nature of migration depends on other factors such as the cultural and economic differences between two countries.

On the whole, the countries of Scandinavia and western Europe are technologically more advanced than the other states of Europe. In the Mediterranean region, we have to make a distinction between Italy and Spain on the one hand and Greece and Portugal on the other. In the latter two countries, the contribution of agriculture to the economy is rather large and they are technologically less advanced than the other EU member states. Spain has been catching up with the EU, in particular after it joined the Union in 1982. Italy is divided into an industrially highly productive northern region and a poor southern region, which lowers its overall performance. The former communist countries can be divided into those that have more or less successfully transforming their economies (e.g. Poland, Hungary and the Czech Republic) and those that are not (e.g. Ukraine, Bulgaria, and Russia). The first group were already relatively wealthy during the communist era, which implies that there is more money for further technological progress. Furthermore, due to their stable financial climate, it is easier for them to attract foreign investors, which further stimulates the state of technology.

2.3 | The Cultural Dimension

Culture refers to the values, norms and customs that an individual learns from society and that lead to common patterns within that society (Assael, 1992). In this study, attention is focussed on the values that influence population dynamics. Being a complex construct, we want to distinguish a number of sub-dimensions of culture, so that we do not have to discuss every element separately. A potential categorisation of the cultural values is given by Inglehart (1990), who states in his seminal work that over the last decades, advanced industrial societies have been characterised by a transition from material to post-material values. An advantage of such a dichotomy is its simplicity, which makes discussions more transparent. A disadvantage is either that only one element of culture is discussed or that different cultural developments (female emancipation, growing individualism) which may have different consequences, are described under a single label. We have therefore opted for a more detailed division of culture in this study to separate the effects of different cultural trends. The additional elements are based on the work of Hofstede (1984), and refer to the fundamental issues societies have to solve. A society's solution with respect to these issues determines a nation's culture. Hofstede, however, assesses the influence of culture within the context of organisational behaviour. As a result, his definitions are not perfectly suited to studying demographic behaviour. We have therefore adapted the definitions on some occasions to make them more suitable for this study. Hence, culture is divided into five elements, namely, (a) power distance, (b) conservatism, (c) gender equality, (d) individualism and (e) post-materialism. The first four elements are based on Hofstede, the last element is based on Inglehart. Instead of conservatism, Hofstede defines uncertainty avoidance as a dimension of culture. We believe that conservatism is a way of dealing with the uncertainties of life. We have to distinguish social conservatism, which refers to the ordering of society, from economic conservatism, which is linked to the ordering of the economic system. Economic conservatism does not necessarily imply social conservatism, which is more important when considering demographic behaviour. For this reason, the terms social conservatism and conservatism are interchangeable in this study.

2.3.1. Power Distance

The factor power distance refers to the distribution of power within society. It has a political component, which distinguishes a democracy where the power distance is relatively small from a dictatorial regime where the power distance is large, and an economic component, which refers to the way in which the economic wealth of a country is distributed. Both from a political and from an economic point of view we may hypothesise that there is a negative relationship between power distance and life expectancy. A democratic government has to satisfy, to some extent, the needs and wants of the electorate in order to be elected. A dictatorial government is more likely to pursue its own goals and tends to be oppressive, which diminishes life satisfaction and may influence life expectancy negatively.

However, the nature of this relationship is not straightforward. For the eastern European countries, we saw a transition from a dictatorial regime to a democracy together with a decline in life expectancy (see e.g. Genov, 1998; Zvidrins, 1998). We therefore conclude that if a more oppressive regime manages the economic resources of a country more efficiently than a democracy it may improve the life expectancy of its inhabitants. This finding is in line with the findings of Inglehart (1990), which show no empirical evidence for a causal relationship between democratic structures and economic prosperity. However, given the same efficiency of the economy, a democracy may lead to a higher life expectancy. In addition, an oppressive regime tends to disturb the economic mechanism as a result of high levels of corruption, nepotism and a lack of institutions whose task it is to distinguish non-profitable from profitable businesses. The current situation in Asia may serve to illustrate that a lack of democracy has negative economic repercussions. Another issue is related to health. Oppressive regimes may achieve fairly good results when fighting relatively simple diseases, but may be less successful in curing diseases like cancer, because their treatment depends on high-quality medical innovations (Guo, 1993). The negative relationship between economic inequality and life expectancy is more direct. Given a similar sufficient average income level, a greater economic power distance implies that a larger proportion of people earn an income that leads to less healthy living conditions. The likelihood of such a scenario depends on the isolation of the economically underprivileged. If an isolated underclass exists, poorer people often have less access to health care systems and consequently their life expectancy decreases.

It is rather difficult to assess the development of power distance, in particular the pattern that developed during the 1990s. Overall, the political power distance in Europe has decreased at a national level. After all, democratic governments replaced dictatorial ones in Greece, Portugal and Spain in the 1970s and in eastern Europe in the 1990s and public institutions were democratised in western Europe in the 1960s and 1970s. In addition, individuals have become more vocal with respect to their governments in western Europe, which may have been caused in part by their higher level of education and the emergence of information networks. However, the democratic structure of European institutions is rather vague and given that more and more issues are being handled by them, it may be argued that at a supranational level, the political power distance has increased. In eastern Europe, the political power distance has decreased but the economic power distance increased following the collapse of communism (Matutinovic, 1998). Given the level of economic inequality in central and eastern Europe and the fact that democratic structures were imposed recently, it may be assumed that the power distance is larger in eastern and central Europe than in the northern, western and southern regions. After all, democracy is not only a matter of institutions but also requires a particular attitude, and it may take time for individuals to acquire such an attitude. For this reason, we also expect that the power distance is larger in southern Europe than in northern and western Europe.

2.3.2. Conservatism

Conservatism may generally be defined as an attachment to traditional values and the belief in a fixed unambiguous set of rules to order society, usually based on the history of a particular society. In this study, we only take into account the indicators of conservatism that are relevant to demographic behaviour such as religious belief, attitudes to abortion and the belief in marriage as the sole institution for family life. Defined in this way, the past decades have been characterised by a steady decline in the belief in traditional structures such as the church and marriage. Inglehart (1990) relates this development to the transition from an agricultural to an industrial society, the introduction of social-security systems and increasing prosperity. These factors diminish the need for fixed structures that provide security, such as traditional marriage. A result of this development is that fewer people choose to marry. Another issue is that marriages today are based on affection rather than on moral commitment, which makes them less stable (Roussel, 1989). A final point is that individuals with extremely conservative religious attitudes are against premarital sex and birth control. As a result, they tend to marry at younger ages and do not have the possibility of planning the number of children.

For these reasons a positive relationship between fertility and conservatism may be hypothesised. Indeed, the decline of the institution of marriage correlates with a decrease in fertility rates (Kuijsten, 1996). In empirical settings, however, a causal positive relationship between fertility and conservatism is hard to find (see e.g. De Jong, 1998). This may be due to the fact that quite extreme levels of conservatism are needed for an effect to be apparent. Most people tend to be moderately conservative, and the effect of this variable may not be noticeable if national-level data are analysed. A related issue is the discrepancy between desirable and actual behaviour. Individuals may have very conservative attitudes but may be more pragmatic in their actual behaviour. Empirical studies show that traditional beliefs may go hand in hand with non-traditional behaviour

(Deutsch and Saxon, 1998). Moreover, the relationship between conservatism and fertility may be non-linear at the national level. In a conservative society, alternatives to marriage may not be available and family planning may be discouraged. This may lead to a higher fertility rate. A progressive society may offer adequate facilities for individuals who favour non-traditional lifestyles, and this may encourage these people to have children. In a nation with moderate levels of conservatism, individuals may favour alternative lifestyles but society may not provide adequate structures to support these lifestyles. For example, women may be stimulated to participate in the economy but childcare facilities may not be sufficient. In that case, the TFR may be lower than in progressive or strictly conservative societies. A positive relationship may be hypothesised between life expectancy and conservatism. Empirical research has shown that people who are married live longer than those who are not. This is probably caused by the fact that negative emotions such as loneliness tend to occur less frequently among married people (Stack, 1998). A family may provide social protection, which can be rather important, especially if the economic climate is bad or uncertain. A negative relationship may be expected between conservatism and migration, especially if we look at the national level. The more conservative a society, the less inclined it will be to accept individuals from other cultures. A large proportion of individuals of foreign descent in a particular society would probably imply social change, which is anathema to conservatives. Hence, perceived cultural differences are relatively large in conservative societies, and this decreases migration.

As mentioned, in recent decades the level of conservatism has decreased in most European countries, in particular in the west and north of Europe. Southern Europe is the most conservative region and the Scandinavian countries are the most progressive, as reflected by, for example, prevailing attitudes towards abortion. The communist regimes repressed religion and as such traditional marriage in a religious sense was uncommon. Moreover, attitudes towards abortion were quite liberal. Following the decline of communism, however, several churches put in an all-out effort to promote traditional family behaviour (for example, in Poland). We may therefore assume that these countries are more conservative than the western and Nordic countries of Europe.

2.3.3. Gender Equality

In modern times, the traditional role of women in society has been to bear and nurture children. Their participation in economic life has therefore been rather limited, accentuating their inferior economic and social status relative to men. In advanced industrial societies, the emancipation of women gained momentum in recent decades. Female labour force participation and women's level of education have increased relative to men. Moreover, non-traditional female gender roles have gained acceptance in recent years. Both the acceptance of non-traditional gender roles and the economic participation of women are important conditions for the total emancipation of women. If non-traditional roles are accepted, but women do not participate in the economy, for whatever reason (e.g. lack of child-care facilities), society is still characterised by economic gender inequality. If non-traditional gender roles are not accepted, women may be kept away from the centres of economic and political power and they may only enter specific segments of the labour market. There is empirical evidence that women take part in specific segments and that these segments are characterised by lower wage levels (Bowlus, 1997). It has been argued that economic equality between men and women precedes social equality (Blumberg, 1984). If that is true, a distinction between social and economic emancipation may be unnecessary. However, though economic participation may be a necessary condition for female equality, it may not be a sufficient one. Moreover, the various combinations of economic and social emancipation may lead to a non-linear relationship between emancipation and the TFR. We have therefore distinguished economic emancipation from social emancipation. Economic emancipation may be reflected merely by the participation rate of females in the economy. Social emancipation is a much broader construct, which may include, for example, the opportunities for women to have managerial jobs, the opportunities for fathers to take parental leave, and the provision of childcare facilities. Although the last element naturally depends on the economic resources of a country, a positive score on this element is indicative of attitudes in favour of gender equality.

Highly developed industrial societies have been characterised by growing economic emancipation over the last century and by growing social emancipation over the past two decades. Emancipation is most advanced in the Scandinavian countries, as reflected by their high ranking on the

Gender Empowerment Index of the United Nations. This index is indicative of the economic and social equality of women relative to men and reveals that the emancipation of women in western Europe tends to focus on economic participation, but that it does not necessarily lead to social equality. Women in these countries often have part-time jobs or are relatively more employed in the lower segments of the labour market. Female emancipation was accepted under the communist administrations of eastern and central Europe, when childcare facilities and the economic participation of women were stimulated. Some researchers argue that the position of women has deteriorated since the fall of communism. Empirical studies, however, do not show a significant decrease in the economic status of women in these regions (Van der Lippe and Fodor, 1998). Women may well participate out of economic necessity. As public spending on childcare facilities has decreased, we may still argue that the inequality between men and women in social terms (i.e. the acceptance of non-traditional gender roles) has increased. This pattern may be stimulated by the growing influence of the church in some countries (in particular in Poland), which stresses the traditional gender roles of females. In sum, it may be argued that today gender equality in central and eastern Europe is lower than in western Europe. The Mediterranean countries and Ireland show the lowest levels of gender equality in Europe. In these countries, traditional religious attitudes (see e.g. Dogan, 1998) are still dominant, hampering the emancipation of women.

The growing emancipation of women may have substantial implications for population dynamics. Increasing labour force participation means that the opportunity costs of having a child will rise. Children do not only lead to immediate cuts in income, but may also harm career perspectives in the long run. The importance of this issue depends not only on the acceptance of female equality as a theoretical ideal, but also on the willingness of society to actively support this goal, i.e. is society willing to change its habits to stimulate gender equality? If society actively embraces the emancipation of women the negative relationship between fertility and gender equality may be quite different. Empirical evidence confirms the hypothesis that economic participation leads to lower fertility (De Man and De Jong, 1997). Increasing emancipation is also correlated with a higher level of education, and this leads to a delay in family formation (Blossfeld, 1995). A negative relationship may exist between emancipation and female life expectancy. As men tend to have unhealthier lifestyles (e.g. more stress, alcohol abuse and smoking) than women, an imitation of a male lifestyle reduces the increase in life expectancy of women relative to men. However, empirical evidence for this relationship is limited. Perhaps the increased mortality may be mitigated by the enhanced life satisfaction of women that results from an increase in economic and social power and growing individual freedom.

2.3.4. Individualism

This element refers to the relationship between individuals and the way they look at their role in society. Do they see themselves primarily as individuals and do they satisfy their own needs rather than the needs of the society they live in or do they consider themselves as a part of a larger society? In this respect, we should distinguish between the desires of people to pursue their individual objectives rather than social objectives and the opportunities they have of doing that. The level of individualism is therefore positively related to GNP as the possibility of exercising an individual lifestyle increases. Still, higher incomes yield higher tax revenues, which in turn may yield more elaborate systems of collective services. The rising status of the free-market economic paradigm in the 1980s together with an increased income level has increased individualism across Europe in the 1990s. However, cross-national differences are still observed; the northern region shows the lowest level of individualism while the southern region has the highest level. In Mediterranean countries such as Spain, individuals often rely on their relatives for support, while in the other regions of Europe, particular in the Nordic countries, they rely on government (Rubery and Smith, 1997). In eastern and central Europe, resentment towards the communist regimes naturally provided a powerful stimulus to increase individualism. However, a lack of social structures tends to harm the economically underprivileged more than it does other groups, and this may induce a return to less individualistic (and probably less democratic) structures if the economic climate remains poor. Such a scenario is not unrealistic given the current popularity of former communist parties in some nations in the eastern and central European regions.

A high level of individualism implies that individual needs are more likely to be fulfilled, as greater efforts can be made to satisfy them. As a result, subjective life satisfaction is higher, and this may have a positive impact on life expectancy (Schyns, 1998; Veenhoven, 1996). A very high level of individualism may, however, result in a weakening of social structures, which may give rise to physical and economic insecurity. We may thus conclude that a moderate level of individualism has a positive effect on life expectancy. A high level of individualism also correlates with a large proportion of single households (Kuijsten, 1996; Van de Kaa, 1987) and may induce a greater need for flexibility. This may lead to an avoidance of long-term commitments such as marriage (Mulder and Manting, 1994). For these reasons, we may expect a negative relationship between individualism and fertility. Individualism stimulates individuals' flexibility and it reduces the value attached to family ties. As a result, people tend to become less attached to their place of birth or their current place of residence. Individualism therefore increases the likelihood of migration. We may therefore expect a positive relationship between individualism and emigration. Having said that, a strong collective system is only sustainable if the group of people who belong to a particular society is well-defined. Along these lines, we may hypothesise a positive relationship between immigration and individualism. The influence of the level of individualism on net migration is thus ambiguous.

2.3.5. Post-Materialism

The basic needs of human beings are food, sex and security, and their primary aim is to satisfy these needs. In advanced industrial societies these needs are likely to be fulfilled. Inglehart (1990) states that over the past decades, these societies have been characterised by a transition from material to post-material values. He defines the need for economic and physical security as materialistic values and the need for belonging, esteem, beauty and intellectual challenge as post-materialistic values. If more and more individuals hold post-materialistic values, it implies that pure economic goals become relatively less important for society and for political action. Instead, non-monetary aspects of the quality of life become more important. Children may be a very important means to realising these post-materialistic values. Indeed, empirical evidence seems to show that having children decreases the feeling of loneliness and hence increases satisfaction in life (Stack, 1998). Schoen et al. (1997) identified couples' motives to have children and found that children may be considered a source of intrinsic, non-substitutable pleasure. Children may also be seen as social capital, i.e. they provide access to critical material resources through kinship ties and other personal relationships (among, for example, parents, grandparents and friends). These motives are in line with those found important in post-materialistic societies. Hence, in such societies, fertility may play a positive, status-enhancing role.

As the quality of life is very important to people who foster post-materialist values, we may assume a positive relationship between the level of post-materialism on the one hand and the fertility rate and life expectancy on the other. Inglehart's study shows that northern and western Europe display higher levels of postmodernism than the Mediterranean countries. This reflects existing differences in economic wealth between these regions. As Mediterranean countries still have a lower level of prosperity, primary needs such as economic security are relatively more important in these countries. They are even more essential in the countries of central and eastern Europe, as the state of the economy is rather unstable in these regions, increasing the need for economic stability.

2.4 | Empirical Analysis of the Determinants

In the previous sections we have theoretically discussed the different dimensions that influence population dynamics. This discussion will be used as a starting point to empirically assess and categorise the countries studied. The aims of this empirical analysis are twofold. Firstly, it is used to validate the two fundamental dimensions underlying the demographic determinants of the two scenarios. Secondly, the results are used to find homogeneous clusters of countries within Europe. In order to keep the discussion as simple as possible, assumptions underlying the scenarios have been formulated for each *cluster* of countries instead of each *individual* country. Having said that, the scenarios will be applied to individual countries, not to clusters of countries.

2.4.1. Data Description

In order to capture the different dimensions discussed in the theoretical section, we collected more than 40 variables for this empirical study. For this purpose, we studied the statistical publications of major supranational organisations, such as the OECD, the World Bank, the WHO, UNESCO and the UN. To avoid further methodological statistical issues, we have mainly used data provided by the ECE (1997). An important reason for using this data source is that data on a large number of variables are available for all the countries studied. A drawback is that the data set lacks attitudinal variables, which makes it more difficult to adequately quantify the cultural dimension. Although cross-national attitudinal data have been collected by some researchers (e.g. Hofstede (1984)) and organisations (The World Value Survey), their data sets were either collected a relatively long time ago, or do not contain all the countries studied, or were not available within a short period of time. This issue has been partially solved by the inclusion of demographic variables that may be regarded as indicators of the cultural dimension (e.g. the divorce rate).

The variables describe the European countries in the period 1993-1995. In about two per cent of the cases, proxies of the values have been used, as some variables were not measured in all countries. In view of the relatively small number of cases used, the lesser data quality of the proxies is not likely to influence the results. In addition, we have performed the analysis with a subset of variables without proximity values, and the results were similar to those of the original analysis. Not all countries for which population scenarios have been constructed, are included in this empirical analysis. Iceland and Luxembourg have been omitted as their small size impedes data collection for a substantial number of variables. Moreover, these nations are likely to produce extreme values, which decreases the stability of the results. *Table 2.1* displays a few key variables for the countries studied. At first glance, these data indicate the vast economic and cultural differences that exist across Europe today. The variables are used to empirically assess the latent dimensions that determine the cultural and economic differences among countries and, therefore, the differences in population dynamics across Europe.

2.4.2. Results

A Principal Component Analysis (PCA) was carried out on several subsets of variables. We use the PCA primarily as a data reduction technique and not to build a confirmatory factor-analysis model. It is not the purpose of

Mellens

Table 2.1. Statistics of a few key characteristic variables for the countries of Europe

Country	Population size (million)	Household size	Female age at marriage	Per capita GNP (US$)	Percentage unemployed	Female participation
Austria	8.05	2.6	26	20.907	3.6	48.1
Belarus	10.3	2.8	21.7	3.972	2.7	59.8
Belgium	10.14	2.5	25.6	20.852	10.2	40.4
Bulgaria	8.4	2.8	22.8	4.62	11.1	47.1
Croatia	4.78	3.1	24.6	3.972	5.2	43
Czech Republic	10.33	2.8	22.4	9.513	3.4	55.8
Denmark	5.23	2.2	29.2	21.502	10.3	71.1
Estonia	1.48	2.4	23.7	4.035	1.8	53.9
Finland	5.11	2.2	27.6	17.188	17.2	55.3
France	58.14	2.5	26.7	19.955	11.6	47.9
Germany	81.64	2.2	27.1	20.37	10.4	48.2
Greece	10.45	2.9	25.1	11.65	10	36.1
Hungary	10.23	2.8	22.2	6.607	9.5	43.8
Ireland	3.58	3.3	27	16.431	12.1	39.7
Italy	57.27	2.8	26.5	19.536	12	34.1
Latvia	2.52	2.6	22.8	3.261	6.6	57.1
Lithuania	3.71	3.2	22.5	4.014	6.1	57.5
Moldavia	4.34	3.2	21.9	1.547	1.4	49.6
Netherlands	15.46	2.3	27.4	19.341	7.1	59.1
Norway	4.36	2.4	27.1	23.202	4.9	64
Poland	38.59	3.1	22	5.478	14.9	51.1
Portugal	9.92	3.2	24.8	12.841	7.2	49.3
Romania	22.68	3	22.4	4.328	8.9	57.9
Russia	148.14	2.8	22.4	4.411	7.9	56.2
Slovak Republic	5.36	2.9	21.3	7.38	12.8	51.5
Slovenia	1.99	3.1	25.4	10.725	7.4	52
Spain	39.21	3.2	26.2	14.216	22.9	36.2
Sweden	8.83	2.1	28.7	18.201	7.6	76.1
Switzerland	7.04	2.3	28	22.4	3.3	55.8
Ukraine	51.53	2.8	22	2.383	0.6	49.6
United Kingdom	58.61	2.5	25.8	18.36	8.6	53.8

Source: ECE (1997)

this study to build an analytical model that explains population dynamics, and the data quality is not good enough to obtain reliable parameter estimates. Several subsets of variables have been used to assess the stability of the results. The scree-test indicates a two-factor solution for nearly all of the factor analyses carried out. Moreover, in the event of a higher-order solution, the interpretation of the third and fourth factors is not straight-forward. For both pragmatic and theoretical reasons, we have opted for a two-factor solution. A VARIMAX rotation has been used to facilitate the interpretation of the factors. Variables of poor data quality or with low loadings on both factors have been excluded, but as mentioned above, this does not affect the conclusions. One factor was found to correlate highly with variables such as the per capita GNP, the percentage of the GNP spent on health, and the percentage of teenage mothers. This factor may reflect the asset (socioeconomic) component of population dynamics. The per capita GNP is directly related to the economic prosperity of a country and the number of teenage mothers may be considered an indicator of a country's health system, in particular of the prevalence of contraception. The amount of money spent on health is an indicator of the health system and of the importance attached to an adequate health system by society.

The second factor is highly correlated with variables such as the labour force participation of women and the number of births outside marriage, which may imply that this factor represents the cultural dimension. Female labour force participation is an important indicator of gender equality, while the number of extramarital births reflects attitudes towards marriage and thus the degree of conservatism of a particular society. Indeed, in societies where traditional marriage is still felt to be important, the number of births outside marriage may be lower than in more secular societies, where a substantial proportion of couples cohabit outside of marriage. Indicators for the level of education load on both factors. Advanced industrial societies require a higher proportion of highly skilled workers and consequently, the inhabitants of such societies remain in education for longer periods of time. However, a higher level of education also leads to a lower level of social conservatism and to the postponement of marriage and family formation. Moreover, an improvement in the social status of women may lead to a higher level of education among women and consequently to a higher mean level of schooling. Another issue is that the percentage of the GNP spent on education is a less reliable indicator of education than the average years of schooling. This may be due to the fact that the actual level of education depends on the absolute amount of money earmarked for this purpose rather than the relative amount. Another interesting result of the analysis is that the rate of inflation and the unemployment level are not adequately described by the two factors. This may reflect the structural nature of unemployment in Europe, which implies that a booming economy does not automatically lead to lower unemployment. Moreover, unemployment seems to be concentrated in particular regions rather than in particular countries. The aggregated national-level data may be too crude to analyse the impact of unemployment. The relationship between the rate of inflation and the state of the economy is non-linear. It is thus less adequately described by a correlation coefficient. A booming economy may give rise to either a cost-pull or a demand-pull inflation due to an excess demand for goods or an increase in wage levels. Still, an economic depression may also coincide with high inflation rates if national central banks try to resolve the situation by increasing the stock of money.

The two factors explain 68 per cent of the cross-sectional variation of the variables. If a larger set of about 20 variables is taken, the two factors still explain 58 per cent of the variation. Since the variables are not an ideal measure for the cultural dimension, and some variables do not have a symmetrical distribution, and since substantial outliers occur, this percentage is quite satisfactory. Linear regression analyses, in which the demographic components are the dependent variables and the factor scores are the independent variables, also show that the two factors have face validity. However, these results are purely descriptive, as the relationship between the two factors and the components may be non-linear. The factor scores are presented in *Figure 2.2*, where the two axes represent the median value of the factor scores. We clearly see a division of the European continent into a Nordic segment comprising the Scandinavian countries, a Roman Catholic cluster with the Mediterranean countries and Ireland, and a western European cluster comprising the remaining western European countries. The former communist countries may be divided into a central European and an eastern European cluster. The socioeconomic factor distinguishes the European Union from central and eastern Europe while the cultural dimension distinguishes the secular from the predominantly Roman Catholic countries. This paper-and-pencil grouping is largely confirmed by a k-means cluster analysis. In sum, we may conclude

Figure 2.2. The factor scores of the European countries

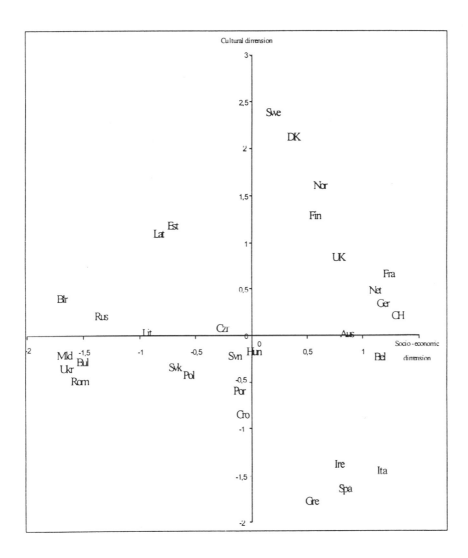

from the empirical analysis that the two broad dimensions, namely the socioeconomic and the cultural dimensions that are described in the literature, are also found in the empirical research. They also provide a workable basis for grouping the European countries and they have adequate explanatory power, given the limitations of the data. Based on these results, we conclude that the two dimensions may be used as a basis for the construction of the scenarios. Note that the empirical analysis only describes the situation today and that we have to make assumptions with respect to the future behaviour of the two dimensions in order to make the scenarios operational. This issue is addressed in the next chapter.

3. Uniformity and Diversity Defined

Martin MELLENS

3.1 | Introduction

On the basis of the dimensions that have been identified in the theoretical and empirical analyses in Chapter 2, a uniformity and a Diversity scenario are constructed. The countries under study are grouped into five different clusters. Each cluster reflects the cultural and economic characteristics dominant for that particular European region and the differences between clusters represent the important economic and cultural differences existing across Europe. In the Diversity scenario, we assume that these cultural and economic differences will persist. In the Uniformity scenario, all European countries will have similar economic and cultural climates in the long run. Arguments in favour of both scenarios are discussed. In this chapter, we will show that currently observed cultural and economic trends lead to these two scenarios. These scenarios may be considered to be feasible outcomes of over-time developments of the two dimensions observed, where convergent tendencies dominate in one scenario whilst divergent developments are dominant in the other.

3.2 | Clustering of the European Countries

The factor analysis results presented in the previous chapter are used to group the European countries into clusters. However, as this analysis only takes into account the present economic and cultural climate and since the

J. de Beer and L. van Wissen (eds.),
European: One Continent, Different Worlds Population Scenarios for the 21ˢᵗ Century, 33–44.
© 1999 *Kluwer Academic Publishers. Printed in the Netherlands.*

scenarios refer to future developments, a number of countries are assigned to other clusters. The categorisation used to construct and discuss the scenarios is set out in *Table 3.1*, where each cluster is named after the cultural climate predominating in that particular cluster.

The different clusters, shown on the map in *Figure 3.1*, are discussed below.

- The *Maternalistic* cluster includes the Nordic countries Denmark, Finland, Iceland, Norway and Sweden. The word maternalistic refers to the relatively high level of female participation in the labour market, the high level of childcare facilities and the fact that female values like co-operation are emphasised in these countries. The majority of these countries are characterised by high per capita GNP, high levels of education and advanced technology. As for their cultural dimension, they show a relatively low level of individualism and conservatism compared to western Europe, especially with respect to family formation, which is reflected by the relatively large number of births outside marriage. Some fertility researchers argue that the United Kingdom should also be part of this cluster and to a certain extent empirical analysis confirms this finding. However, the similarity between the United Kingdom and the Nordic countries in the empirical analysis is partly due to the similarity in the number of births outside marriage. Other empirical research, however, shows that individuals in the United Kingdom have more conservative attitudes to family formation (Harding, Phillips and Fogarty, 1986) and abortion (Scott, 1998).

Table 3.1. Assignment of the countries to the five cultures

Cluster	Countries
Maternalistic	Denmark, Finland, Iceland, Norway, Sweden
Pragmatic	Austria, Belgium, France, Germany, Ireland, Luxembourg, Netherlands, Switzerland, United Kingdom
Paternalistic	Greece, Italy, Portugal, Spain
Intermediate	Croatia, Czech Republic, Estonia, Hungary, Latvia, Lithuania, Poland, Slovak Republic, Slovenia
Post-totalitarian	Belarus, Bulgaria, Moldova, Romania, Russia Ukraine

Figure 3.1. Countries and clusters in Europe

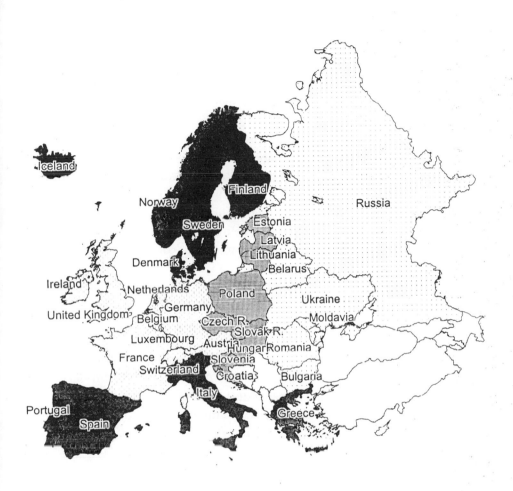

Europe
clusters of countries

- ■ northern cluster (5)
- □ western cluster (9)
- ▨ southern cluster (4)
- ▦ central cluster (9)
- □ eastern cluster (6)

Moreover, the age-specific fertility rates follow a different pattern in the United Kingdom (Coleman and Chandola, 1998). For these reasons, we conclude that the United Kingdom is culturally distinct from the Nordic countries and we assign it to the western European region.

- The *Pragmatic* cluster consists of the western European countries. In this region, economic wealth is of prime importance (in particular economic growth) both at macro and micro levels. Cultural aspects of society are handled pragmatically so that they do not impede economic performance. As a result, these countries tend not to obtain extreme scores, especially with respect to gender roles and conservatism. Female emancipation and alternative lifestyles are accepted, but there is neither encouragement nor any active policy to achieve complete equality. Although at present Ireland is still a traditional Roman Catholic nation, it is assumed that in the future Ireland will have a culture of pragmatism because it has experienced strong economic growth and is very attractive to multinationals. These developments link it more closely to western Europe and we therefore assume that Roman Catholic values will become less pronounced over time.

- The Mediterranean countries are attached to the *Paternalistic* cluster. The term paternalistic refers to the prevalence of traditional family values, the lack of female emancipation and the low level of childcare facilities. Consequently, this culture scores high on conservatism and low on gender equality. Portugal has been assigned to this cluster, although the factor analysis suggests that it bears greater similarity to central European countries. In particular, Portugal scores higher in the cultural and lower in the socioeconomic dimension than other Mediterranean countries. This is mainly due to the fact that agriculture plays a more important role in the Portuguese economy than in other European countries. Thus, average income in Portugal is quite low compared to other EU countries. As a result, the level of education is also quite modest, which may lead to the relatively high proportion of teenage mothers and births outside marriage. Hence the higher score in the cultural dimension may be due to the lack of economic development rather than female emancipation. In addition, the economic participation of females is relatively higher in societies where agriculture is important. It may also be due to socialist experiments (the nationalisation of important industries) which took place after military dictatorship ended in the 1970s. However, in 1982 Portugal joined the European Union, which stimulated reforms towards a more liberal economy. We may assume that the Portuguese economy will catch up with other EU countries, in particular with the Mediterranean states, in which case the contribution of the agricultural sector may be reduced. Moreover, like Italy and Spain, the majority of Portuguese are Roman Catholics, which may be quite an important determinant of demographic behaviour. It is for these reasons that we assign Portugal to this cluster rather than to the Intermediate group.

- The *Intermediate* culture is dominant in the countries of central Europe. These former communist countries are relatively modern and share a non-communist history between the two world wars during which democratic governments were installed. Thus they are culturally more closely related to Western Europe and economically they are relatively more prosperous than the states in eastern Europe. Indeed, Inglehart (1990) states that these countries would have changed to a capitalist system at the end of the 1970s if there had been no threat of a Soviet invasion. Nevertheless, these countries are less wealthy than the countries in northern, western and southern Europe and a substantial number of people in central Europe still hold neo-communist views, which is reflected in the large size of the communist party compared to the EU standard. Moreover, there is considerable environmental impact due to the importance accorded to industrial output combined with the use of less efficient technologies.

- The *Post-totalitarian* culture is characterised by an incomplete transition to a capitalist structure in the sense that it is not rooted in a firm legal and cultural structure (see e.g. Russia). This implies that although superficial democratic institutions may exist, effective political and economic power remains in the hands of a small group. The power distance in this region is therefore large in both economic and political terms. Female participation in the economy is high, of necessity, but this does not lead to an acceptance of non-traditional gender roles.

3.3 | Uniformity and Diversity Scenarios

3.3.1. Uniformity versus Diversity

Today, there are still vast differences in both cultural and economic dimensions across European countries. Nevertheless, developments indicating the increasing integration of European countries have also been observed. In western Europe a decrease in traditional values such as religious belief, nationalism and authority (Dogan, 1998) has been detected. Economies also tend to integrate and there is some empirical evidence that European economies are in a state of convergence (Beine and Hecq, 1998). We may assume that this trend will continue increasingly rapidly due to the introduction of a single European currency. Educational attainment levels have risen in all European countries and students are increasingly able to attend university abroad. Moreover, the quality of the education system is related to the economic prosperity or GNP of a country, so that the former converges if the latter does too (OECD, 1996). The OECD has noted that the total amount of money spent on education expressed as a percentage of GNP is similar across member countries (OECD, 1996).

The cultural dimension's trend towards uniformity may be explained by the transition from material to post-material values, as a result of increasing levels of wealth observed in many advanced industrialised countries (Inglehart, 1990). The diffusion of cultural values is facilitated by the growing number of globally operating multinationals and the increasing importance of global mass media (e.g. Internet, global broadcasting systems). Individuals need to share some values in order to work together or understand foreign broadcasting programmes. The diffusion of values is also due to a decrease in perceived distances because of relatively low travelling costs and a growing awareness of issues which can only be solved on a supra-national scale (e.g. green-house effects, international crime). There is empirical evidence from cross-cultural research that individuals across countries do not hold completely different values, but merely rank these values differently. If cultural differences are based mainly on different rankings, the diffusion of cultures is not unrealistic. The existence of global brands with effective global advertising campaigns also indicate diffusion of cultures. Nowadays, brands do not just have tangible assets such as a particular quality level, but they are also powerful phenomena emphasising a particular lifestyle. Brand image is emphasised by advertising campaigns and the fact that similar campaigns are effective across different countries expresses the existence of some similarity of cultural values across countries. It has also been shown that teenagers all over the world exhibit similar consumption patterns (Assael, 1992), which increase the likelihood of future cultural diffusion. Given the above, cultural and economic developments in different countries and thus demographic developments may converge. In addition to this economic and cultural convergence, some researchers have underlined that particular demographic variables show similar patterns in different countries and that these developments sometimes converge (see e.g. Morris, 1997; Shim, 1998). For example, all advanced industrialised nations have experienced a decline in fertility, an increase in life expectancy and a decrease in household size. In the Uniformity scenario, we assume that the convergent tendencies dominate, leading to a situation where socioeconomic and cultural differences are reduced substantially. Consequently, the trends in the demographic components that are influenced by these socioeconomic and cultural dimensions also converge.

The rather optimistic Uniformity scenario makes the assumption of increasing political integration and easy diffusion of cultural values. And for the former communist nations, it assumes successful transition from a communist to a capitalist economy. Coleman (1997) lists the assumptions in the Uniformity scenario and concludes that it is doubtful whether they could all be satisfied. It has also been shown that similar demographic patterns may have different sources (Caplow, 1998; Day, 1995; Kuijsten, 1996; Rodrik, 1998). This implies that convergent behaviour in the past does not necessarily imply future convergence. Local customs, in particular those supported by cultural values, are likely to be strong and may not change rapidly. In addition, a nation's culture may be shaped by cultural values which are often country specific and which result partly from a country's historical development and dramatic events (e.g. war). For example, Inglehart (1990) found a substantially lower level of life satisfaction in those countries on the losing side in the Second World War. Given that history is never the same for any two countries, we may argue that there always will be cultural differences, the importance of which is emphasised by the fact that despite the popular talk about global branding among marketing managers, firms still add local features to their marketing efforts to optimise their sales. Indeed, denying cultural differences may turn out to be a fundamental marketing mistake, as evidenced by the initial failure of Eurodisney (Hartley, 1995). Even though France and the United States are both advanced industrialised nations, individuals in the two nations had different ways of spending their leisure time and had different price perceptions.

If a more detailed examination of the socioeconomic dimension is made, two observations can be noted: significant differences in per capita GNP and regional differences which do not converge within some countries (Siriopoulos and Asteriou, 1998). This appears to show that wealth transfer is not easily achieved, despite a similar culture. Geographical differences may make it more efficient for industries to locate in a specific region. If such an industry is characterised by low labour productivity, then according to classical economic theory, that region will have a lower per capita GNP. Since different nations may specialise in different industries, technological development may also be unevenly spread, because some industries are more prone to technological innovations (e.g. computer industry) than others (e.g. services). Moreover, the adoption of new technologies may depend on situational country-specific characteristics. If adequate substitutes for new technologies are available, older techniques may be used for quite some time (Landes, 1969). Thus we may argue that there will be substantial economic differences between different regions of Europe. These contrasts in turn may affect education and health systems, which already show substantial differences across countries. Although the amount of money spent on education would appear to converge, the organisation of the education system differs across countries, which in turn causes differences in the effectiveness of education. Thus in this view we opt for a Diversity scenario in which clusters of countries in Europe will be significantly different as regards their cultural and economic characteristics. As a consequence, these different regions show varying demographic patterns.

3.3.2. An Operational Definition of the Uniformity Scenario

The Uniformity scenario assumes that the cultural and economic differences between European regions will decrease substantially or even vanish. A supra-national economic market will develop within Europe and all European countries will become European Union members. There are no barriers to labour mobility, goods and capital. The disappearance of cultural differences will stimulate labour mobility and may create a more flexible labour market. Thus a similar culture is a necessary condition for an optimal economic market. In turn, economic integration will stimulate cultural integration due to workers in different countries co-operating and the existence of global broadcasting stations and globally operating multinationals. The diffusion of workers from different countries may play a prominent role in the diffusion of cultural values. Some level of political integration will also further an efficient economic market, as policy makers provide a legal framework within which economic agents can operate. In order to achieve this aim, both at national and supra-national (EU) levels, democratic structures have to be created. A firm legal structure should be confirmed by a mandate of the European countries' residents. Otherwise, laws will not be obeyed or will be evaded, and this would weaken the conditions necessary for an efficient economic market. This is why the Uniformity scenario is characterised by a smaller political power distance as a result of the emergence of democratic structures.

High economic growth, stimulated by international free trade, will be achieved by a high rate of technological progress. This may be achieved by better diffusion of new technologies and by the growing availability of capital. This will lower interest rates, stimu-late investment and hence technological progress. Moreover, lower barriers will stimulate economic competition within Europe, which will force firms to rapidly adopt new technologies. This diffusion of technologies will enable the economically backward areas of Europe to catch up with the leading economies, which may also develop under normal circumstances, but as their initial level is higher, it is harder to make substantial progress. The level of education is also likely to increase over time and a learning effect may improve workers' skills. As a result of technological progress and higher education levels, labour productivity will increase, resulting in higher income levels. The increase in income may make individuals more aware of the things they want, including non-materialistic values like a sense of belonging. Hence, people may spend relatively less money and effort to achieve materialistic goals. Such a scenario is in line with statements made by several researchers (Coleman, 1997; Inglehart, 1990). This trend is even stronger as a result of the higher level of education, since having a higher educational attainment seems to be correlated with the importance of post-material values (Inglehart, 1990). An increasing equality between men and women is assumed in the Uniformity scenario, which is partly the result of an increasing level of education among women. Moreover, the past decline of fertility rates will cause future labour market shortages. Women will have to participate in the economy in order to maintain economic growth. They will increasingly participate in non-traditional jobs and so economic participation will in turn lead to social emancipation. This shift to a more complete concept of emancipation together with increasing economic prosperity leads to relatively high quality childcare facilities.

3.3.3. An Operational Definition of the Diversity Scenario

In the Diversity scenario, economic and cultural differences between clusters persist, although it is assumed that there will be convergence within clusters. The within-cluster convergence in this Diversity scenario may be attributed to the assumption that in the long run differences in demographic behaviour which cannot be attributed to economic and cultural dimensions will disappear. Obviously, the validity of this assumption is questionable. It does not seem very likely that each country within a cluster will be identical in terms of demographic behaviour. Nevertheless, this assumption is justified as we aim to identify structural differences in demographic behaviour that may prevail in the long run rather than claim to be able to distinguish all possible sources of future demographic differences between separate countries. Differences across countries may either stem from country specific characteristics, or be the result of temporary differences between countries, or might simply be random fluctuations. The impact of these variables is of little import in this study. Instead, we are concerned with the average influence of feasible cultural and economic developments on the population pattern.

Political integration will be limited in the Diversity scenario, which hampers the free market and consequently economic and technological growth. We assume there are three socioeconomic and five cultural patterns. One socioeconomic pattern applies to the European Union countries, i.e. the Maternalistic, Materialistic and Paternalistic clusters. The countries in these regions that are not part of the EU are closely linked to the economic situation in the EU, so that it is not unrealistic to expect their socioeconomic development to be strongly linked to the EU pattern. With the introduction of the Euro, resulting amongst other things in increased harmonisation of economic policies, we assume that economic developments in the EU countries converge to a common pattern. Yet, even though in this scenario EU economic growth is the highest in Europe, it is lower than the growth rate obtained in the Uniformity scenario. Cultural barriers hamper the free market and the diffusion of technological innovations. A different development applies to the countries in the post-totalitarian cluster. One can argue that political reforms will be incomplete, which will hamper economic growth. Uncertainty of the political situation will also discourage foreign investment. Moreover, capital flight may occur because it is more profitable for Russian bankers to invest their capital abroad. As a result, technological progress will lag behind and result in relatively low labour productivity and income. The poor economic climate will also lead to a middling quality medical system, compared to other parts of Europe in particular. A third pattern is related to the countries in the Intermediate cluster. Their economic performance is better than that of the eastern European states, but lags behind economic growth in the EU (see e.g. The Economist, 1998). There is also a major impact on the environment due to the emphasis on industrial output combined with the use of less efficient technologies. For example, the use of brown coal in central European countries has led to a very high atmospheric concentration of sulphur dioxide. All these factors will lead to a lower socio-economic dimension score than in the EU countries.

Some of the cultural patterns of each cluster have already been described in section 3.2 when we discussed the clustering of the European countries. We do not expect their cultural characteristics to change significantly in the future. The Maternalistic cluster will have the highest level of gender equality and the lowest level of individualism, although these levels may tend to approach the western Europe levels as a result of the current free-market economic paradigm. On the other hand, the economic and social position of females will continue to be marginal relative to men in the Paternalistic cluster. Due to lower economic growth, there is not enough money available for adequate childcare facilities. In the Pragmatic cluster, economic progress will continue to be the most important element. In the popular press, there seems to be a call to return to traditional values, and remarks that growing individualism is harming social welfare. Hence we may expect the level of conservatism to rise and the level of individualism to decrease. Due to the ageing population, females' economic participation must increase and consequently we expect economic inequality between males and females to continue to erode. In the Post-totalitarian cluster, democratic reforms will be superficial and so the power distance will be large in political and economic terms. Since individuals cannot rely on the government, individualism will rise. In addition, government expenditure will decrease and this will further dismantle childcare facilities. For economic reasons, females will continue to participate in the labour market, but they lack the option of satisfactorily combining their economic role and family life. In the Intermediate cluster, power distance and individualism are situated between the eastern European and western European levels. Given the better economic outlook for, and the democratic history of this region, democratic structures are more deeply rooted in society than in eastern Europe. Nevertheless, these countries are less wealthy than the countries in northern, western and southern Europe and a substantial proportion of people will hold communist views, which is realistic given the large size of the communist party in this region compared to the EU standard.

4. Uniformity and Diversity Scenarios for Fertility

Andries DE JONG and Rob BROEKMAN

4.1 | Introduction

Population dynamics are still largely determined by long-term trends in fertility, despite the growing importance of (net) migration in many European countries in recent decades. The development of fertility has shown drastic changes since the Second World War. Fertility levels were initially well above replacement level, generally surpassing pre-war levels. This led to the post-war baby boom.

In the northern, western and southern regions of Europe, economic reconstruction was accompanied not only by rapid technological changes and growing prosperity but also by profound societal changes and a loosening of sexual morals, giving rise to sustained high fertility levels up to around the mid-1960s. A dramatic fall in birth rates over a period of about ten years led to the virtual disappearance of large families. Two children became the generally desired family size. Although more and more women stayed childless in their twenties, this was not seen as the ideal. In the wake of women's liberation, the period during which women pursue an education has been prolonged. To reap the benefits of their higher level of education, a rising number of women are active in the labour market and they have increasingly postponed the decision to have a baby until after the age of 30 when fears of possible infecundity come into play. In most western European countries the total fertility rate has remained more or less constant since the mid 1970s, resulting from the

J. de Beer and L. van Wissen (eds.),
European: One Continent, Different Worlds Population Scenarios for the 21st Century, 45–69.
© 1999 Kluwer Academic Publishers. Printed in the Netherlands.

combination of a tendency to delay motherhood at relatively young ages and to catch up at more advanced ages. In the southern European countries the course of fertility was determined primarily by the postponement of childbirth, leading to unprecedentedly low fertility levels in the absence –until recently– of the catching-up effect. The northern European (maternalistic) countries showed a modest upswing in fertility in the second half of the 1980s, followed by a sudden fall in Sweden and rather stable levels in the other Scandinavian countries.

The era of communist regimes in central and eastern Europe was characterised by pronatalist policies. Favourable conditions were created to allow women to combine motherhood and labour force participation. As a result, total fertility was generally at or above replacement level in the 1970s and 1980s. However, since the late 1980s, the countries of central and eastern Europe have been involved in a transition from a centrally planned economy to a market economy. A deep economic recession and social disruption accompanied this process and fertility plummeted to historically low levels. Due to the limited availability and awareness of modern contraceptives, these low birth rates were predominantly the result of abortion. In some countries, the number of abortions exceeded the number of live births. In sharp contrast with the northern, western and southern regions of Europe, the fertility of women in central and eastern Europe reached its peak in the early 1920s as a result of the initiation of sexual life at young ages and the tradition of early marriage.

4.2 | Differences in Fertility Trends between European Countries

Europe's current fertility is among the lowest in the world, with about 1.5 children per woman, compared with two children in North America and nearly six children in Africa (Van der Gaag et al., 1999). All the countries of Europe have seen their fertility rates fall during the course of the 20th century. Still, important differences persist across Europe.

4.2.1. Northern Europe (Maternalistic Cluster)

The Scandinavian countries may be considered to be forerunners in fertility trends, combining high labour force participation with high fertility in the

late 1980s. The northern countries have seen a marked expansion of the welfare state over the past twenty years. A main feature of this development has been the expansion of the educational system. As a result, the proportion of highly educated women has increased rapidly. The rise in educational attainment also triggered a rise in participation rates. A strong attachment of women to paid employment will tend to postpone maternity. However, a relatively high fertility among women in their thirties, due to a catching-up effect, counterbalanced the decrease in fertility rates at young ages. Several authors (Ellinsæter and Rønsen, 1996; Hoem, 1993; Sundström and Stafford, 1992) draw attention to the tax and family policies in the northern countries, which stimulate both fertility and women's paid work by reducing the costs of having children. In 1974 Sweden became the first country to give both mothers and fathers the right to paid leave from work at childbirth. Other important policy measures encouraging women to combine children and a job are subsidised day care, flexible working hours, economic support to families with children and a progressive tax structure in combination with separate taxation of spouses. Rubery and Smith (1997) speak of the Nordic model, which may be labelled 'everyone a breadwinner', as all fit adults of working age, whether they are mothers or not, are likely to be employed or looking for work.

4.2.2. Western Europe (Pragmatic Cluster)

Fertility trends in western Europe have been far from uniform, resulting in relatively low fertility levels in Germany and Austria on the one hand and relatively high levels in France, Ireland and the United Kingdom on the other. This disparity may be explained by the large variability across these countries in the institutional arrangements enabling women to combine employment and parental responsibilities. Despite the establishment of fairly generous family policies such as child allowances and maternity leave in Germany and Austria, childcare facilities seem to be underdeveloped. According to Höhn (1991b), businesses in Germany ignore the needs of parents and children, while Nebenführ (1995) stresses that the majority of Austrians are in favour of better day-care facilities. Rubery and Smith (1997) say these countries belong to the strong male breadwinner model, based on the assumption of a male breadwinner and a dependent wife. Both Germany and Austria now have the lowest fertility levels of all western European countries.

In France, the level of service provision is high, particularly for childcare. A coherent system of measures in favour of families and birth promotion was launched in this country as early as 1939 and up to the present day many forms of financial support are used to stimulate childbirth (Pressat, 1991). The current high level of fertility in Ireland may be in Ireland may be attributed to the influence of the Catholic church. However, in the wake of a transformation process from an agricultural economy to a modern economy, characterised by capital-intensive industries, fertility is falling rapidly.

4.2.3. Southern Europe (Paternalistic Cluster)

All southern European countries have experienced a period of sustained, fairly rapid fertility decline since the early 1970s. This decline is related to the changing status of women as a result of their greatly improved level of education and employment. Women today seek a social status based on labour force participation and the related financial rewards (Chesnais, 1996). Having several children implies the risk of being condemned to the old-fashioned role of a housewife. According to Golini and Nobile (1991) the family planning strategy of couples in Italy is based on rationality and hedonism, stimulated by the lack of financial support for families. Tax deductions and family allowances are very low. Their standard of living is thus markedly reduced by the arrival of children. In Spain, too, couples today want to live more comfortably than previous generations. They therefore tend to postpone childbearing until a reasonable degree of job security has been reached, given high levels of youth unemployment (Martin, 1992).

A country's housing policy may also lead to the postponement of childbearing. According to Arango and Delgade (1995) high costs of housing have been a factor in explaining the decline in nuptiality and, as most births take place within marriage in the southern countries, the decline in fertility. Castiglioni and Zuanna (1994) point out that public housing has barely been developed in Italy. In a market with high prices, many young couples therefore postpone living together.

Despite the extremely low fertility level, attitudes towards the family and parenthood appear to be very favourable in Italy (Palomba, 1995). The high appreciation of parenthood could, paradoxically, explain the low birth rate: rather than having several children, Italians prefer to have only one child, becoming the sole object of much care and attention.

4.2.4. Central and Eastern Europe (Intermediate and Post-totalitarian Clusters)

Under communism, the central and eastern countries developed various common policies which were different from those in the northern, western and southern regions of Europe. So it may come as no surprise that the fertility trends of the central and eastern European countries (including former East Germany) are very similar. Up to the late 1980s, the pro-natalist policies of the communist states were quite successful, leading to relatively high fertility rates. In the early 1990s, the transition from a centrally planned economy to a market economy led to a fall in birth rates at an unprecedented speed.

During the communist era, family formation was characterised by both high first marriage rates and early marriage. Early marriage was partly encouraged by these countries' housing policies, as young single people had little chance of obtaining a home of their own. Moreover, early marriage was the only way in which young people were able to become independent from their parents (Kocourková, 1997). Another critical factor in the relative attractiveness of marriage was the absence of personal opportunities outside the family (Ní Bhrolcháin, 1993). Having children hardly curtailed women's opportunities, since government policy was oriented at combining motherhood with work outside the home through measures such as maternity benefits, child allowances and generous childcare provisions.

The economic recession following the collapse of communism in the late 1980s led to massive cutbacks in childcare provisions. Social reforms created greater personal freedom for individuals. A new situation has emerged for women, who now have to choose between motherhood and other options. Due to the meagre and declining job prospects combined with the virtual disappearance of childcare provisions, women are starting to see having children as a social and financial risk (Beck-Gernsheim, 1997). In countries with high divorce rates, such as Latvia (Zvidrins,

1998), women who become lone mothers are particularly prone to deprivation. Faced not only with more options in life but also with more risks and uncertainties, having children is no longer taken for granted and women have started to postpone childbearing, in expectation of better times.

4.3 | Fertility Prospects for Europe

The second half of the 20th century has been characterised by profound socioeconomic and cultural changes. With respect to women's role in society, the increasing level of education and the upswing in labour force participation are two major structural changes. In countries where these phenomena have been supported by the state, such as the provision of parental leave and day-care centres to reconcile work and family obligations, fertility levels have remained high or have even recovered. In countries where government policy has not been supportive of families, and in countries where childcare provisions have been cut back due to severe economic problems, fertility levels are expected to plummet.

There appears to be no consensus among demographers with respect to future trends in fertility. Bosveld (1996) has positioned countries on a modernisation track. She states that all countries are following the same trajectory, albeit with time lags. The Maternalistic Scandinavian countries are leading the way: these countries show modern behaviour with respect to the regulation of fertility and the possibility of combining employment and family life. The western Pragmatic countries trail behind northern Europe on the modernisation track, showing various elements of modern behaviour. In the southern European countries of the Paternalistic cluster women's behaviour in this area has long been traditional, but changes have recently taken place. In the Intermediate and Post-totalitarian countries of central and eastern Europe we find a mixture of modern and traditional behaviour: a high labour force participation rate of women goes hand in hand with a high marriage rate and a limited use of modern contraceptives. Bosveld places the southern, central and eastern European countries in an earlier phase of the modernisation trajectory.

Day (1995) expects that fertility in the 'developed' countries of the world will increase to close to replacement levels. The countries with the sharpest declines in fertility were those with the highest fertility levels at the start. The very fact that in these countries fertility has reached historically low values supports the prospect of an increase, or at least a minor rise. This increase will presumably take place in response to government policy but a renewed emphasis on the family and parenthood is also possible. Greater emotional value may be attached to children as large numbers of men and women are finding that they receive insufficient emotional gains from their work, neighbourhood and religion.

According to Coleman (1996) new patterns of family formation and living arrangements have appeared in Europe. Having said that, the rate at which different populations have adopted these patterns differs greatly, thereby creating renewed diversity in fertility trends after a long period of convergence. As yet, European values, attitudes and behaviour with regard to fertility are not uniform. Still, based on conventional socioeconomic models of fertility, a greater similarity between European countries may be expected following the convergence of economic and welfare arrangements within the European Union. Kuijsten (1996), too, perceives substantial between-country variations and a significant degree of dynamics in family patterns. He speaks of a pluralisation of living arrangements in Europe and points at different structural conditions, that is to say strong cultural and psychological factors which influence both family forms and family policy. In his view, the situation in Sweden does not necessarily predict the future situation in the other countries of Europe. According to Chesnais (1996) contemporary western European societies may be subsumed under one of two categories: 'nations of families' or 'nations of individuals'. An unstable pattern of differences exists as all countries are experiencing rapid social change, reflecting a clash between tradition and modernisation. As a result, attitudes and public policies regarding the family may be distinctly different across countries.

In view of the opinions and arguments presented above, two separate scenarios for future fertility trends emerge. One scenario envisions a modernisation process, in which all countries are on the way to a fertility rate approaching replacement level, while the other scenario stresses the structural economic and cultural differences between European countries, prolonging the diversity in fertility trends.

4.4 | Fertility Scenarios

4.4.1. Method

The key assumptions of the Uniformity and Diversity scenarios have been formulated on the basis of the cultural and economic dimensions of fertility behaviour. The assumptions have been specified in both qualitative and quantitative terms. In translating the qualitative assumptions into quantitative assumptions, the Total Fertility Rate (TFR) has been used as the main indicator of future fertility behaviour. As modern fertility trends are closely connected to processes such as delaying motherhood at young ages and catching up at older ages, a second key indicator has been used, namely the average age at childbirth. The TFR equals the sum of age-specific fertility rates measured in a particular calendar year. Hence, it is a period indicator of fertility and changes in the TFR are due to both changes in the average number of children per woman as well as to changes in the timing of childbirth. It is for this reason that the TFR in the central and eastern regions of Europe fell so rapidly in the early 1990s: women postponed childbearing and, depending on future economic and social prospects, this may end in them not having children at all. Although the TFR is a period indicator of fertility, in situations where age-specific fertility rates hardly change over a rather long period of time (20 or more calendar years), it can also be considered an approximation of the average number of children per woman.

The quantitative assumptions of the scenarios involve the specification of both a target level and an average age at childbirth for the two scenarios and for each of the five clusters of countries. Moreover, it has been assumed that these targets will not be reached in the same time horizon. Hence, the target year might not be the same in both scenarios and across all clusters. In general, the following line has been followed: the larger the gap between the latest observed figure and the target level, the later the target year will be. However, the target year is the same for all countries within a specific cluster. In addition to the fertility level an age pattern of fertility is specified for the target year. For the intermediate years between the last observation and the target year an age-specific curvilinear path is set out, after which age-specific fertility rates are kept constant. *Table 4.1* presents the recent trends and fertility assumptions for both scenarios.

Table 4.1. Total fertility rate

	Observed				Uniformity scenario			Diversity scenario		
	1975	1985	1995	1997	2000	2025	2050	2000	2025	2050
North										
Denmark	1.9	1.4	1.8	1.8	1.8	1.8	1.8	1.7	1.6	1.6
Finland	1.7	1.6	1.8	1.8	1.8	1.8	1.8	1.7	1.6	1.6
Iceland	2.6	1.9	2.1	2.0	2.0	1.8	1.8	1.9	1.6	1.6
Norway	2.0	1.7	1.9	1.9	1.8	1.8	1.8	1.8	1.6	1.6
Sweden	1.8	1.7	1.7	1.5	1.6	1.8	1.8	1.5	1.6	1.6
West										
Austria	1.8	1.5	1.4	1.4	1.4	1.8	1.8	1.4	1.5	1.5
Belgium	1.7	1.5	1.5	1.6	1.6	1.8	1.8	1.6	1.5	1.5
France	1.9	1.8	1.7	1.7	1.8	1.8	1.8	1.7	1.5	1.5
Germany	1.5	1.4	1.2	1.4	1.5	1.8	1.8	1.4	1.5	1.5
Ireland	3.4	2.5	1.9	1.9	1.9	1.8	1.8	1.8	1.5	1.5
Luxembourg	1.5	1.4	1.7	1.7	1.8	1.8	1.8	1.7	1.5	1.5
Netherlands	1.7	1.5	1.5	1.6	1.6	1.8	1.8	1.6	1.5	1.5
Switzerland	1.6	1.5	1.5	1.5	1.5	1.8	1.8	1.5	1.5	1.5
United Kingdom	1.8	1.8	1.7	1.7	1.7	1.8	1.8	1.7	1.5	1.5
South										
Greece	2.3	1.7	1.3	1.3	1.4	1.7	1.8	1.3	1.4	1.4
Italy	2.2	1.4	1.2	1.2	1.3	1.7	1.8	1.2	1.4	1.4
Portugal	2.6	1.7	1.4	1.5	1.5	1.7	1.8	1.5	1.4	1.4
Spain	2.8	1.6	1.2	1.2	1.3	1.7	1.8	1.2	1.4	1.4
Central										
Croatia	1.9	1.8	1.6		1.7	1.8	1.8	1.7	1.3	1.3
Czech Republic	2.4	2.0	1.3	1.2	1.2	1.6	1.8	1.2	1.3	1.3
Estonia	0.0	0.0	1.3	1.2	1.3	1.6	1.8	1.3	1.3	1.3
Hungary	2.4	1.8	1.6	1.4	1.4	1.7	1.8	1.4	1.3	1.3
Latvia	2.0	2.1	1.3	1.1	1.2	1.6	1.8	1.2	1.3	1.3
Lithuania	2.2	2.1	1.5	1.4	1.4	1.6	1.8	1.4	1.3	1.3
Poland	2.3	2.3	1.6	1.5	1.4	1.6	1.8	1.4	1.3	1.3
Slovak Republic	2.5	2.3	1.5	1.3	1.4	1.6	1.8	1.4	1.3	1.3
Slovenia	2.2	1.7	1.3	1.4	1.3	1.6	1.8	1.3	1.3	1.3
East										
Belarus	2.2	2.1	1.4	1.2	1.3	1.6	1.8	1.2	1.1	1.1
Bulgaria	2.2	2.0	1.2	1.1	1.1	1.6	1.8	1.1	1.1	1.1
Moldavia	2.6	2.7	1.8		1.6	1.6	1.8	1.5	1.1	1.1
Romania	2.6	2.3	1.3	1.3	1.4	1.7	1.8	1.3	1.1	1.1
Russia	2.0	2.1	1.3		1.3	1.6	1.8	1.2	1.1	1.1
Ukraine	2.0	2.0	1.4	1.4	1.3	1.6	1.8	1.3	1.1	1.1

4.4.2. Uniformity Scenario

In the Uniformity scenario a similar economic and cultural climate will emerge across Europe. This development will lead to an improvement of the basic conditions under which people have children. The economy will develop favourably and people will have confidence in the future. Family incomes will rise and sooner or later couples will be able to have the desired number of children. Positive economic developments will create an increasing demand for labour. Female labour force participation will increase, reinforced by an increase in the level of education. As women stay in education for longer periods of time and pursue professional careers, childbearing will be delayed more and more. This may result in permanent childlessness, as infecundity is markedly higher at older ages. Good childcare provisions and generous parental leave schemes may counterbalance this negative effect of economic prosperity on fertility. Hence, economic growth may go hand in hand with high fertility when women are able to combine motherhood with a paid job. This requires not only sufficient facilities such as childcare and flexibility in working arrangements, but also a more equal distribution of responsibilities between men and women. Both partners in a couple are expected to participate in the task of raising children. If norms and values are still based on the idea of a male breadwinner and a dependent wife, this is set to change in the wake of the process of emancipation.

Another important change needed to secure reasonably high fertility levels is the improvement of the housing situation in large parts of Europe. High housing costs or the unavailability of appropriate houses prevent many of today's couples from living together and having children. This will change as governments give greater priority to housing policies.

The quantitative specification of the Uniformity scenario is based on the assumption that the economic and cultural conditions in this scenario allow couples to have their desired family size. Based on an analysis of fertility surveys in several countries of the European Union, Van Hoorn and Keilman (1997) show that among young women the average expected number of children is just above two children. However, this does not imply that in this scenario the TFR will reach a level of slightly above two. Empirical studies show that realised fertility tends to be somewhat lower. One reason is infecundity. The tendency to postpone fertility will continue and lead to an average age at motherhood of thirty years. Many couples will face the fact that infecundity will prevent their childbearing intentions from coming true. In addition, the break-up of relationships may impede the realisation of the desired level of fertility. Furthermore, some couples may adapt their expectations as they postpone having children. The actual ultimate number of children will thus be 1.8 rather than two per woman.

The countries of the northern European (Maternalistic) cluster have had a TFR of about 1.8 since the early 1990s. The relatively high fertility level of this cluster may be related to the existence of an elaborate system of childcare provisions and family regulations. Budget constraints due to the economic recession may, however, pose a threat to this system. The rapid fall of the TFR in Sweden in the mid-1990s may be explained by cutbacks in the most generous measures. The Uniformity scenario assumes that an economy recovery will ensure the sustainability of family-friendly policies. As a result, the countries of the Maternalistic cluster will have reached the target level by 2020 at the latest.

In the countries belonging to the western European (Pragmatic) cluster, the degree to which government policies are family-friendly differs sub-stantially. This may explain the rather large variability in present-day fertility levels. In several countries a change in attitude is needed to permit women to adopt the modern pattern of combining work and parenthood. For this reason it will take more time for them to reach the target level and the countries that lag behind will not reach this level before 2025. In the southern, central and eastern European clusters, a large gap between current fertility and the target level has to be bridged. In the southern (Paternalistic) countries, family-friendly policies have yet to be introduced, while the economic and social disruption that has accompanied the fall of communism in the central (Intermediate) and eastern (Post-totalitarian) countries, has led to the erosion of childcare provisions. The route towards a modern and prosperous welfare state is expected to be long, and this explains why 2050 has been taken as the year in which a TFR of 1.8 will be reached.

4.4.3. Diversity scenario

The Diversity scenario assumes that socioeconomic and cultural disparities between countries will continue to influence fertility in Europe. Economic growth will slow down in the northern, western and southern regions of Europe whereas in the central and eastern regions economic prospects are expected to remain gloomy. Governments and the corporate world will cut expenses and there will be insufficient resources for childcare facilities and parental leave. Couples will gradually loose confidence in the future. Because the costs of raising children are high, more and more women will decide to stay childless or to have only one child at most. The average age at motherhood will rise, as the majority of women will wait for better times. In uncertain and depressing circumstances, people tend to hold onto traditional structures, so traditional family formation and lifestyles are set to persist.

In the countries of the western (Pragmatic) cluster a rather large diversity in fertility levels exists, the TFR varying between 1.4 (Germany and Austria) and 1.9 (Ireland). In the Diversity scenario, the TFR of the western cluster is assumed to move towards 1.5. This value has been calculated by taking the weighted group average and the estimated negative effect of gloomy economic prospects on fertility. For most western countries, this value points to a downward trend in the future. However, for some low-fertility countries, this value implies a slight increase, based on the assumption that the process of delaying childbirth will gradually slow down as fertility is already very low among women of young generations. This downward effect on the TFR will be more than offset by a catching-up effect, a process that has just started among women of older generations and that is set to accelerate in the future. As in the Uniformity scenario, the calendar year 2025 has been taken as the latest year in which the target value of 1.5 will be reached.

For the northern (Maternalistic) cluster, budget deficits are expected to endanger the sustainability of the generous provisions enabling women to combine motherhood and a job. This will lead to cutbacks in the elaborate system of family provisions. As a result, the TFR is set to drop from about 1.8 to a level of 1.6. The pruning of the welfare system will be a gradual process as each austerity measure will meet social and political opposition.

The decrease in fertility will also be gradual and this process is set to come to a halt in 2030.

In the southern (Paternalistic) countries, women delayed childbirth in the 1980s and early 1990s and many women now face involuntary child-lessness. Traditional norms and values still prescribe that people start a family, if not a large family –in true Catholic tradition– then at least a one-child family. So, the process of postponement will gradually slow down and be accompanied by a catching-up process. As a result, the TFR will slowly rise from a value of just above one to a level of 1.4, which will be reached in 2030.

In all Intermediate and Post-totalitarian countries in central and eastern Europe fertility has fallen drastically since the early 1990s. However, the pace of the decrease has been far from uniform. Many countries are approaching a TFR of one while others have values comparable to those of the countries in western Europe. The countries of eastern Europe have been hardest hit by social and economic disruption and their populations will have to cope with lasting unfavourable conditions for couples who want to have children. In the face of harsh times, women will have an average of no more than 1.1 child. Although the situation in central Europe is far from perfect, the countries of this cluster are assumed to benefit from the remnants of the socio-cultural infrastructure left by past democratic governments that ruled before communism took over. The economies of some countries are already recovering and social disruption is less intense than in eastern Europe. For this reason, the TFR is somewhat higher than in eastern Europe and a TFR of 1.3 has been assumed in the Diversity scenario. The stagnation of economic growth in both central and eastern European countries will prevent a rapid rise in the TFR. Hence, their target levels will not be reached before 2030.

In northern, western and southern Europe the average age at childbirth will continue to rise and is set to reach a value of 30. This trend is primarily due to a process of postponement. Youngsters are prolonging their stay in the educational system to get better qualifications for a job. Moreover, after having acquired a job they first want to set aside savings to be able to meet the financial requirements of having children. In eastern and central Europe, the tradition of early marriage and childbirth will have a lasting influence, although this trend is expected to abate somewhat. Women in these two clusters will have children (or rather, their first and only child) at an average age of 28.

4.4.4. Fertility Differences between the Uniformity and Diversity Scenarios

The results of the assumptions of the two scenarios differ among the five clusters. In order to give a concise presentation of the main differences, only one country has been taken to represent each cluster. In Norway, the exemplar of the northern (Maternalistic) European countries, the difference in the TFR between the two scenarios is relatively small (*Figures 4.1-4.3*). However, a look at age-specific trends reveals larger disparities. This is not the case for the age group 15-24 where, under both scenarios, the observed downward trend will continue into the future. Among women aged 25-29, where the gradual decrease of the 1990s is expected to continue in both scenarios, the differences are also marginal. Important developments are apparent in the over-30 age group: fertility has risen since the second half of the 1980s and an acceleration of this upswing is visible in the early 1990s. The Uniformity scenario assumes a sustained rapid rise while the Diversity scenario assumes that the upward trend will level off.

Despite rather large differences in the TFR across the western European (Pragmatic) countries the age-specific trends are more or less the same. Germany represents the western cluster (*Figures 4.4-4.6*). The process of postponing fertility at young ages is apparent in all western countries and this is set to continue in the future under both scenarios. Fertility among women aged 25-29 showed a rather stable development over the past 25 years. It is worth mentioning that this is the result of a combination of falling fertility rates at younger ages and rising rates at older ages. Under both scenarios the fairly stable development will be sustained, although at a slightly different level. In some countries, e.g. France and the United Kingdom, the process of catching-up started in the latter half of the 1980s while in other countries the process did not start until recently. Both the Diversity scenario and the Uniformity scenario depict a continuation of the process, albeit at a much faster pace in the Uniformity scenario.

In the southern (Paternalistic) countries, the TFR fell from relatively high levels to historically low levels. Only recently did this process seem to have ended. Spain has been taken to illustrate these developments (*Figures 4.7-4.9*). Fertility rates among young women are already very low and will not fall any further in the future. Also among women aged 25-29 no further fall is foreseen. In the Diversity scenario the current level will continue in the future, while in the Uniformity scenario a return to higher levels is foreseen. Among 'older' women, both scenarios point to a catching-up process, albeit more strongly in the Uniformity scenario.

The Czech Republic serves as an example of the fertility trends in Intermediate central Europe (*Figures 4.10-4.12*). The pronatalist policy of the communist regime led to a TFR of about 2.0. After the collapse of communism, the TFR fell to unprecedentedly low levels. Today, fertility is still reasonably high at young ages and both scenarios foresee a further fall in the future. Fertility among women aged 25-29 is set to rise somewhat. However, the large future rise in the TFR under the Uniformity scenario is predominantly caused by the 30-plus age group. Although fertility trends per age group are more or less the same in the Diversity scenario, there are some important differences. In this scenario women aged 25-29 will continue to have the highest fertility rates. The rise in fertility among women aged 30 and over will be much smaller than in the Uniformity scenario and will be just enough to offset falling fertility at younger ages. As a result, only a slight rise in the TFR is expected in the future.

Observed fertility trends in the eastern European (Post-totalitarian) countries resemble those of the Intermediate cluster. Russia (*Figures 4.13-4.15*), too, experienced a steep fall in fertility in the 1990s. The Diversity scenario assumes that the disruptive effects of the transition from a centrally planned economy to a market economy will be stronger than in the countries of central Europe due to the absence of a firm legal and cultural structure. Here, a modest upswing in fertility rates at older ages is not enough to offset the drastic fall in fertility rates at younger ages. As a result, the process of delaying childbirth will eventually lead to higher childlessness. Under the Uniformity scenario, favourable economic developments will result in an increase in fertility rates. The decline in fertility at young ages will be followed by an increase at older ages.

Figure 4.1. Total fertility rate, Norway

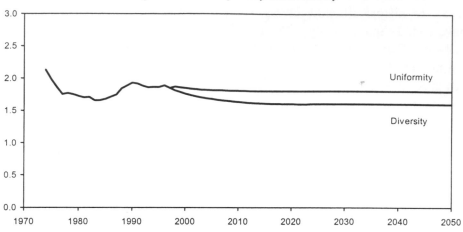

Figure 4.2. Age-specific fertility rates, Norway (x 100)

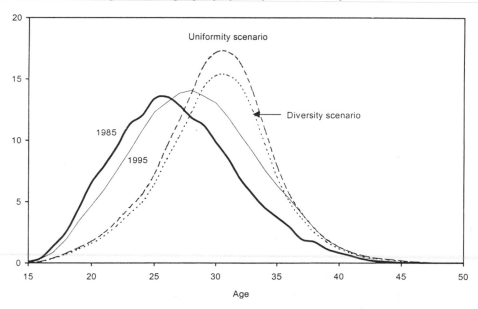

Figure 4.3. Sum of age-specific fertility rates per age group, Norway (x 100)

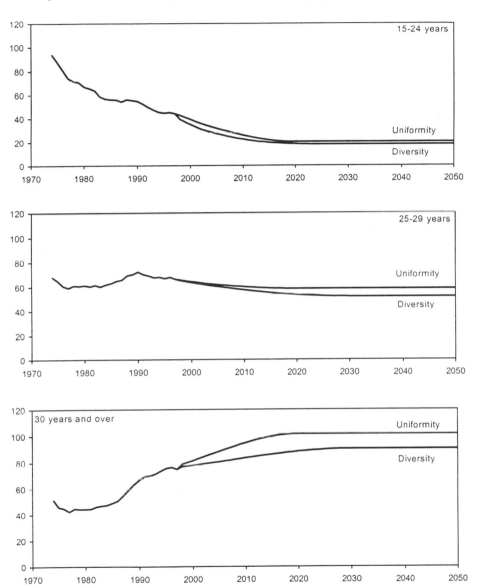

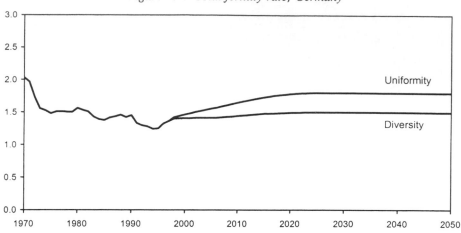

Figure 4.4. Total fertility rate, Germany

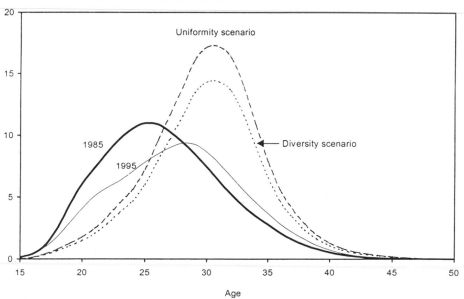

Figure 4.5. Age-specific fertility rates, Germany (x 100)

Figure 4.6. Sum of age-specific fertility rates per age group, Germany (x 100)

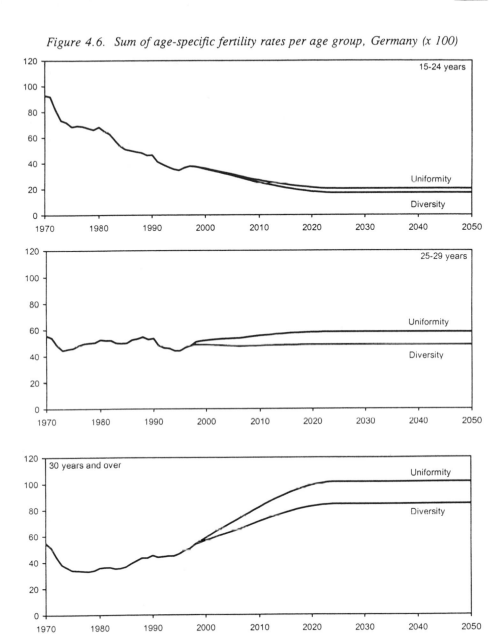

Figure 4.7. Total fertility rate, Spain

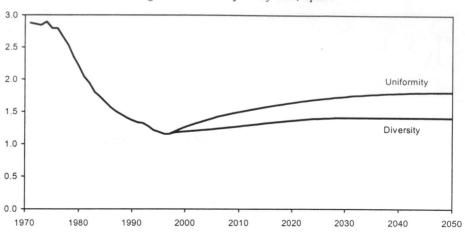

Figure 4.8. Age-specific fertility rates, Spain (x 100)

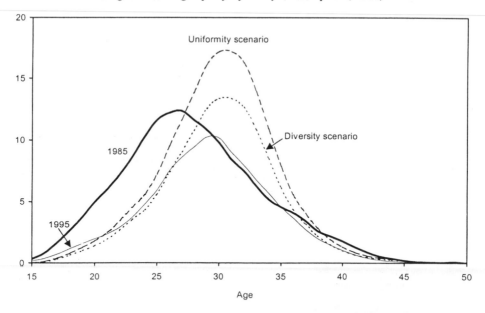

Figure 4.9. Sum of age-specific fertility rates per age group, Spain (x 100)

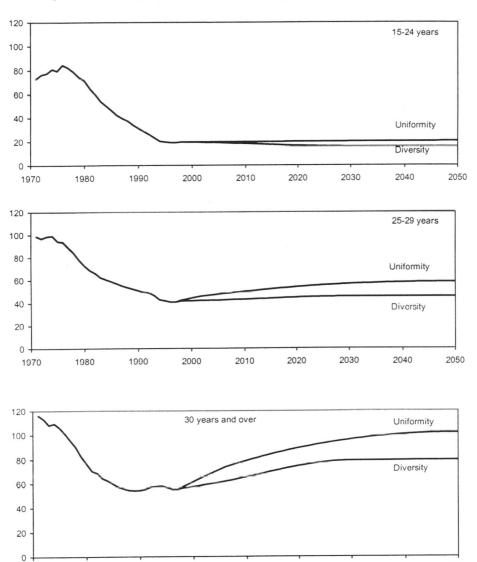

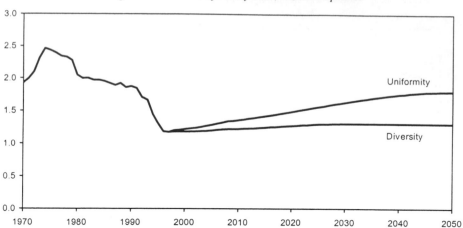

Figure 4.10. Total fertility rate, Czech Republic

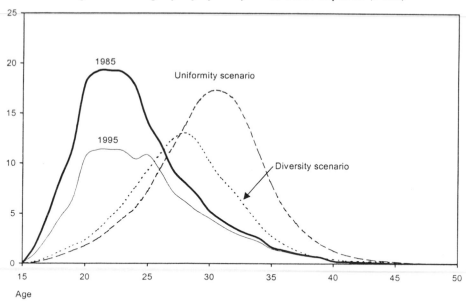

Figure 4.11. Age-specific fertility rates, Czech Republic (x 100)

Figure 4.12. Sum of age-specific fertility-rates per age group, Czech Republic (x 100)

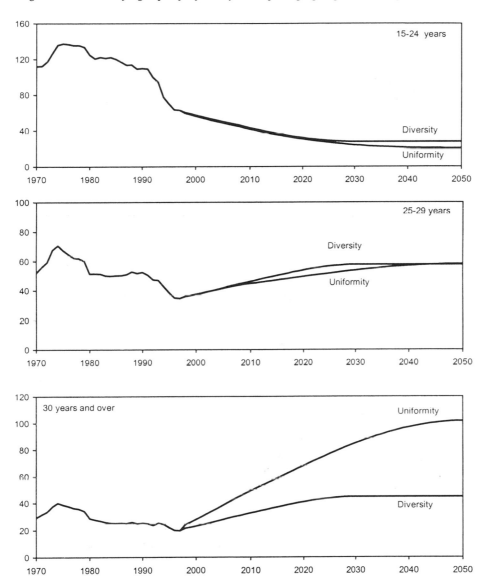

Figure 4.13. Total fertility rate, Russia

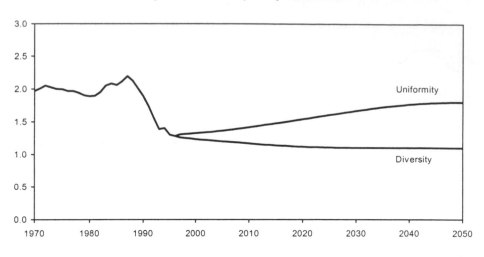

Figure 4.14. Age-specific fertility rates, Russia (x 100)

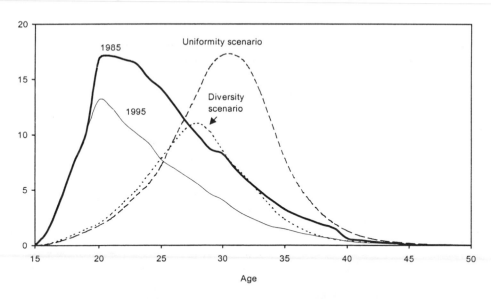

Figure 4.15. Sum of age-specific fertility rates per age group, Russia (x 100)

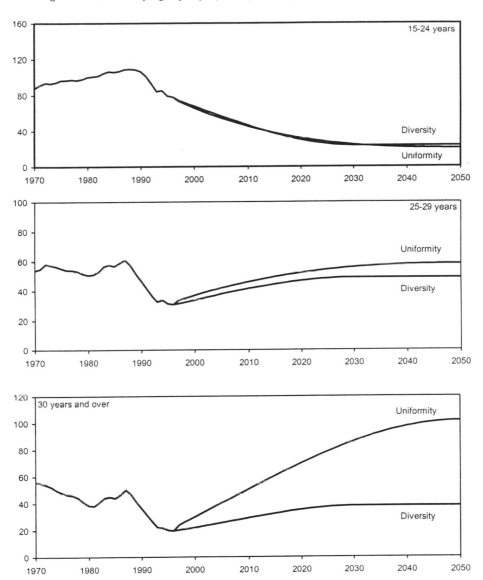

5. Uniformity and Diversity Scenarios for Mortality

Wim VAN HOORN and Rob BROEKMAN

5.1 | Introduction

Mortality has changed dramatically during the course of the 20th century. Contagious diseases have been almost wiped out by vaccines and antibiotics. This has caused a tremendous decrease in mortality rates, especially among young people, and has consequently led to a large increase in life expectancy. Most deaths today concern elderly people and occur following a chronic disease (most frequently heart disease and malignant neoplasms).

In the period 1950-1970, the development of mortality was rather similar in western and eastern Europe. Life expectancy increased for both sexes until 1960. In the 1960s, male life expectancy stagnated. But after 1970, mortality trends in western and eastern Europe differed considerably. Whereas male life expectancy started to increase once again in western Europe, in most eastern European countries no progress was made and since the 1980s a number of countries have even shown a decline. In western Europe diseases of the circulatory system at middle-to-old ages were successfully combatted, and to a lesser extent malignant neoplasms and other diseases. Eastern Europe, however, showed no or only little improvement (see, for instance, Guo, 1993 or Mesle and Hertrich, 1997). Furthermore, female life expectancy has been increasing less strongly.

J. de Beer and L. van Wissen (eds.),
European: One Continent, Different Worlds Population Scenarios for the 21st Century, 71–90.

5.2 | Differences in Mortality between European Countries

5.2.1. Northern, Western and Southern Europe

Since 1970, life expectancy at birth has increased in all countries of the European Economic Area. However, there are considerable differences in the rate of increase. Male life expectancy has increased most strongly in Austria, Finland and Portugal. There has been relatively little increase in Denmark. In the Netherlands, Norway and Sweden, too, the increase in life expectancy was below average. Life expectancy of females has risen sharply in all countries of southern Europe, but much less so in Scandinavia and the Netherlands. One explanation may be that in countries with relatively high mortality rates, progress can be made more easily than in countries with comparatively low mortality, such as in Scandinavia, where new positive factors are needed for further progress. As a result, the differences in life expectancy between northern, western and southern Europe have diminished considerably since 1970.

Until the mid-1980s, the average decline in mortality rates of women exceeded that of men. Hence, the gap in life expectancy widened. Over the last ten years, however, the gender gap has narrowed. In northern, western and southern Europe, fairly similar developments in gender differences are visible –a widening of the gap followed by convergence– but the timing of the trend differs. In the north, the gender gap started to narrow before 1980, whereas in western Europe this did not set in until recently. In southern Europe the gap is still widening. It may thus be concluded that for both sexes mortality is converging in the European Economic Area, caused primarily by considerable progress in southern Europe.

If mortality is distinguished by cause of death, we see that a very striking development has taken place in death by lung cancer: since 1970 there has been an increase. In total mortality this has partly offset the positive development of other causes of death. For both sexes mortality rates by lung cancer have increased dramatically by several hundred per cent. For women, the increase started later than for men. In Finland and England a peak was reached for males around 1980. Since then, mortality by lung cancer has declined in these countries. Italy and France have probably reached their peak about now, whereas Portugal will not reach its maximum mortality by lung cancer before the turn of the century.

Suicide rates have also risen in recent decades, but to a much lesser extent than deaths by lung cancer. Fatal road accidents increased sharply until the 1970s, but have since declined almost to the 1950-1954 level. This trend is remarkably uniform across Europe. This decline may be attributed to the introduction of speed limits, regulations regarding seat belts and crash helmets, road improvements and information campaigns. In general, the different causes of death show fairly similar developments in the various European countries, but the timing of the trends differs.

5.2.2. Central and Eastern Europe

Most experts believe that there is a direct link between the negative trends in mortality in eastern Europe and the poor socioeconomic climate in this region. In their opinion, the collapse of the communist system gave rise to a state of material and moral breakdown, which had a very negative effect on many aspects of life and, consequently, on mortality. Zvidrins (1998) describes the current situation in Latvia. It appears that more than 80 per cent of the decrease in life expectancy in 1991-1994 was due to a mortality increase in working ages. Excessively high rates of cardiovascular dis-eases, lung cancer, respiratory problems and accidents are caused by a high prevalence of risk factors such as smoking, alcohol abuse (which has increased dramatically), violence and inappropriate nutrition, such as highly saturated fats and environmental pollution. More or less the same factors are mentioned by Notzon et al. (1998), who have analysed recent developments in Russia. They also draw attention to the deterioration of the health care system, such as deficiencies in modern medical equipment, and poor health education. Genov (1998) describes how a weakening of social integration in Bulgaria has resulted in the deterioration of the quality of life and subsequently a decrease in life expectancy.

However, trends in the former communist countries are not uniform, some performing better than others. The former Soviet countries, among them the Baltic states, are doing far worse than the central European countries such as the Czech Republic (see e.g. Coleman, 1997). Since 1989, mortali-ty levels in the Czech Republic have improved significantly and the enormous gender differences have narrowed somewhat. Infant mortality has declined by about 40 per cent. There has been a substantial decrease in circulatory disorders in the age group 40-79. Underlying factors may be detected at both the individual and the macro level (Kocourková, 1997). Individuals have been given greater responsibility for their own health and more freedom to choose which doctors and medical facilities they wish to use. Modern medical equipment and medication are now available. Furthermore, programmes have been implemented to upgrade the natural environment.

The Balkan countries, such as Slovenia and Croatia, are also doing comparatively well. Around 1950 they had very low life expectancies, but in the period 1950-1990 these countries experienced a rise in life expectancy.

The importance of economic factors in explaining the negative mortality trends in the former communist states of eastern Europe may be confirmed by the experience in some areas of western Europe where similar negative economic developments have taken place. In regions with outdated industrial infrastructures, such as central England, the Ruhr region in Germany and northern France, mortality has developed rather negatively. High unemployment in combination with poverty and an unhealthy lifestyle are believed to be the major causes of these trends (Van Hoorn and De Beer, 1998).

The behaviour of men, in particular, was adversely affected by the socio-economic decline of communist societies. As for purely economic factors, women and men are likely to be affected in the same way, for instance as a result of inadequate diets, poor housing, unfavourable environmental conditions and a deteriorating health care system that is increasingly being eroded by a serious lack of materials and supplies. However, apart from occupational risks which tend to be higher for men, some other gender-related factors appear to be important. For instance, in a recession, men's behaviour appears to be affected much more strongly than that of women. In deteriorating economic circumstances and mass unemployment, men often lose their self-esteem and are inclined to succumb to unhealthy lifestyles, such as alcohol abuse. Women, on the other hand, in particular those who have a family, generally succeed in maintaining a responsible way of living. A parallel may be found in the socioeconomic differences within western Europe, which are clearly larger among men than among women (Valkonen, 1994).

5.2.3. Main Differences

As a result of these divergent trends, large differences in current mortality exist between the former communist countries in central and eastern Europe and the rest of Europe. Mortality differences between the countries of northern, western and southern Europe are small and, moreover, seem to be due in part to coincidence.

In the vast majority of the northern, western and southern countries, female life expectancy exceeds 80 years, but this figure is not reached in any of the countries of central Europe and in eastern Europe a female life expectancy of 75 years is reached only in Bulgaria (*Table 5.1* and *Figure 5.1*). The difference for males is even larger. Whereas in the northern, western and southern European countries male life expectancy is about 74 years, in central Europe it is 65 to 70 years and in eastern Europe 60 to 65 years (again, Bulgaria has a higher figure, about 68 years).

On average, life expectancy of males in the northern, western and southern regions is slightly lower than female life expectancy in central Europe and slightly higher than female life expectancy in eastern Europe. The average female life expectancy in the northern, western and southern regions is just under five years higher than in central Europe and somewhat more than five years higher than in eastern Europe.

5.3 | Mortality Prospects for Europe

Differences of opinion exist between scientists with very optimistic views about future longevity and experts who are more pessimistic. The pivotal question is whether or not there is a fixed biological limit to human life (for instance, 115 years which seems to be the figure nowadays). If ageing is seen as an intrinsic process in all human cells, a maximum life span is likely (Duchene and Wunsch, 1991). If one sees ageing as a multi-dimensional process of interaction in which partial loss of function in one organ is synergistically compensated by other organs, life span would not

Table 5.1a. Life expectancy at birth, males

	Observed				Uniformity scenario			Diversity scenario		
	1985	1990	1995	1997	2000	2025	2050	2000	2025	2050
North										
Denmark	71.5	72.0	72.7	73.2	73.9	79.4	83.0	73.7	77.6	80.0
Finland	70.1	70.9	72.8	73.3	74.0	79.5	83.0	73.7	77.5	80.0
Iceland	74.8	75.4	75.9	76.4	76.9	80.8	83.0	76.5	78.8	80.0
Norway		73.4	74.8	75.4	76.2	80.9	83.0	75.7	78.3	80.0
Sweden	73.8	74.8	76.2	76.7	77.1	80.8	83.0	76.8	78.8	80.0
West										
Austria	70.4	72.4	73.5	74.2	74.8	79.8	83.0	74.6	78.0	80.0
Belgium	71.1	72.7	73.4	73.9	74.6	79.8	83.0	74.3	77.9	80.0
France	71.2	72.7	73.9	74.2	75.1	80.1	83.0	74.8	78.2	80.0
Germany		71.9	73.2	73.7	74.4	79.7	83.0	74.1	77.9	80.0
Ireland			73.0	73.5	74.2	79.7	83.0	73.6	76.9	80.0
Luxembourg		72.3	72.6	73.2	73.9	79.5	83.0	73.6	77.7	80.0
Netherlands	73.1	73.8	74.6	75.0	75.6	80.1	83.0	75.3	78.3	80.0
Switzerland		74.0	75.3	76.0	76.5	80.5	83.0	76.1	78.6	80.0
United Kingdom			74.0	74.4	75.1	79.9	83.0	74.8	78.1	80.0
South										
Greece	73.5	74.6	75.1	75.1	76.0	80.5	83.0	75.7	78.5	80.0
Italy	72.3	73.6	74.9	74.9	75.8	80.4	83.0	75.5	78.5	80.0
Portugal	69.3	70.4	71.2	71.8	72.6	78.9	83.0	72.4	77.2	80.0
Spain	73.1	73.3	74.3	74.8	75.4	80.2	83.0	75.1	78.3	80.0
Central										
Croatia				70.5	71.3	78.2	83.0	70.6	73.3	75.0
Czech Republic			69.7	70.5	71.2	78.1	83.0	70.6	73.3	75.0
Estonia				65.2	66.2	75.2	83.0	65.6	71.0	75.0
Hungary			65.2	66.5	67.3	76.2	83.0	66.7	71.7	75.0
Latvia				64.1	65.9	77.5	83.0	65.0	72.6	75.0
Lithuania			63.5	65.3	66.6	77.6	83.0	65.7	72.0	75.0
Poland				68.5	69.6	77.9	83.0	68.8	73.1	75.0
Slovak Republic			68.3	68.9	69.9	77.6	83.0	69.2	72.8	75.0
Slovenia			70.7	71.3	72.1	78.6	83.0	71.3	73.7	75.0
East										
Belarus				62.9	64.4	75.4	83.0	63.2	67.4	70.0
Bulgaria			67.4	68.0	69.1	77.2	83.0	67.8	69.2	70.0
Moldavia				63.3	64.6	75.7	83.0	63.3	67.5	70.0
Romania				65.0	66.9	77.2	83.0	65.5	69.2	70.0
Russia				61.0	62.4	74.9	83.0	61.3	66.7	70.0
Ukraine				59.9	61.5	74.2	83.0	60.4	66.7	70.0

Table 5.1b. Life expectancy at birth, females

	Observed				Uniformity scenario			Diversity scenario		
	1985	1990	1995	1997	2000	2025	2050	2000	2025	2050
North										
Denmark	77.5	77.7	77.8	78.2	78.9	83.4	86.0	78.3	81.3	84.0
Finland	78.7	78.9	80.2	80.3	81.0	84.1	86.0	80.7	82.8	84.0
Iceland	80.4	80.6	79.6	81.3	80.8	84.1	86.0	80.4	82.2	84.0
Norway		79.8	80.8	81.0	81.5	84.4	86.0	81.1	82.7	84.0
Sweden	79.7	80.4	81.4	81.8	82.1	84.6	86.0	81.7	82.9	84.0
West										
Austria	77.3	78.9	80.0	80.5	80.9	84.1	86.0	80.5	82.3	84.0
Belgium	78.0	79.4	80.2	80.5	81.1	84.2	86.0	80.6	82.3	84.0
France	79.4	81.0	81.9	82.1	82.5	84.8	86.0	82.1	83.1	84.0
Germany		78.4	79.7	80.0	80.5	84.0	86.0	80.1	82.1	84.0
Ireland			78.6	79.0	79.6	83.7	86.0	79.1	81.7	84.0
Luxembourg		78.6	79.8	80.2	80.8	84.2	86.0	80.4	82.4	84.0
Netherlands	79.7	80.1	80.4	80.7	81.1	84.2	86.0	80.7	82.4	84.0
Switzerland		80.7	81.7	82.2	82.4	84.7	86.0	82.0	83.0	84.0
United Kingdom			79.2	79.6	80.1	83.8	86.0	79.6	81.9	84.0
South										
Greece	78.4	79.5	80.3	80.6	81.0	84.1	86.0	80.6	82.4	84.0
Italy	78.7	80.1	81.2	81.3	81.9	84.6	86.0	81.5	82.9	84.0
Portugal	76.4	77.4	78.6	78.9	79.4	83.4	86.0	79.0	81.5	84.0
Spain	79.6	80.4	81.5	81.7	82.1	84.6	86.0	81.7	82.9	84.0
Central										
Croatia				77.3	78.0	83.0	86.0	77.2	79.0	80.0
Czech Republic			76.7	77.5	77.9	82.7	86.0	77.4	78.6	80.0
Estonia				75.8	76.6	81.7	86.0	75.9	78.0	80.0
Hungary			74.5	75.0	75.9	82.0	86.0	75.2	77.5	80.0
Latvia				74.9	75.8	81.7	86.0	75.4	78.3	80.0
Lithuania			75.1	75.6	76.4	82.2	86.0	75.5	77.7	80.0
Poland				77.0	78.0	82.9	86.0	77.2	78.7	80.0
Slovak Republic			76.4	76.7	77.5	82.6	86.0	76.7	78.4	80.0
Slovenia			78.3	78.7	79.2	83.4	86.0	78.4	79.3	80.0
East										
Belarus				74.3	75.2	82.0	86.0	74.5	76.8	78.0
Bulgaria			74.8	75.2	75.9	81.6	86.0	75.0	76.5	78.0
Moldavia				71.0	72.3	80.8	86.0	71.5	76.4	78.0
Romania				73.0	74.0	82.0	86.0	73.5	76.7	78.0
Russia				73.1	74.1	81.6	86.0	73.4	76.1	78.0
Ukraine				71.9	72.9	81.0	86.0	72.4	76.4	78.0

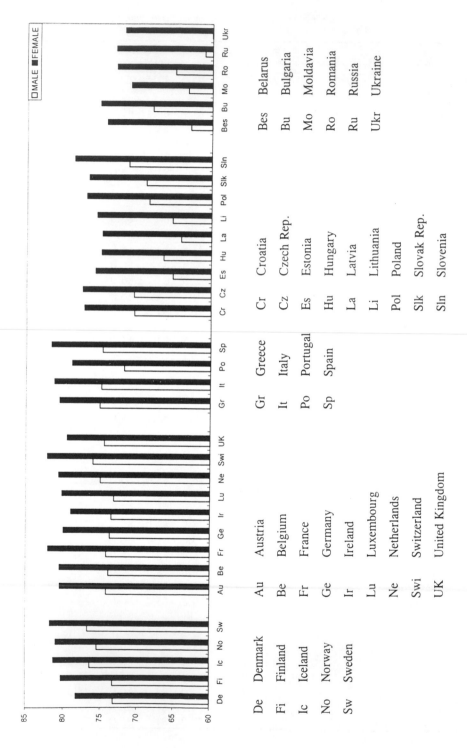

Figure 5.1. Life expectancy at birth, 1997

De Denmark
Fi Finland
Ic Iceland
No Norway
Sw Sweden

Au Austria
Be Belgium
Fr France
Ge Germany
Ir Ireland
Lu Luxembourg
Ne Netherlands
Swi Switzerland
UK United Kingdom

Gr Greece
It Italy
Po Portugal
Sp Spain

Cr Croatia
Cz Czech Rep.
Es Estonia
Hu Hungary
La Latvia
Li Lithuania
Pol Poland
Slk Slovak Rep.
Sln Slovenia

Bes Belarus
Bu Bulgaria
Mo Moldavia
Ro Romania
Ru Russia
Ukr Ukraine

☐MALE ■FEMALE

have a fixed limit. Only total failure or loss of a necessary organ system would result in death. Future advances in technology, in particular gene techniques, have the potential of greatly extending our life span (Manton, 1991). However, apart from the question whether new advances in medicine will be far-reaching and imminent, it is not certain whether all individuals would benefit from new bio-technologies. The costs may well be very high. Painful decisions in the health care system are already being discussed, such as decisions about the selection of persons who are eligible to receive human transplant organs.

Furthermore, new threats to life may come from new virulent diseases for which no cure or immunisation is available or from old diseases for which the existing treatments are no longer effective. At this moment, death rates of the oldest old are not improving much in some European countries, and in some cases they are even rising. Even if the major causes of death (cancer and heart disease) were to be eliminated, gains in life expectancy would be moderate (Olshansky et al., 1990). So without real breakthroughs in medicine, longevity is not set to rise very much.

In view of these arguments, a moderate increase in life expectancy may be expected in all countries that have already reached low levels of mortality, whilst in the other countries progress may be greater. The exact magnitude of this increase and the pace at which it will take place is uncertain, however.

In the short term, not all diseases are set to benefit to the same degree from improvements in health care services, progress in medical knowledge and from healthier lifestyles. For instance, there has been little progress in finding a cure for most cancers and a breakthrough is probably still far-off. Since a large number of genes and mutations of genes seem to be connected with cancer, only a very gradual reduction in cancer mortality is likely to be achieved. In the short term, gene therapy will be most successful for a number of rare diseases. So far, nobody has really been cured thanks to gene therapy, though efforts have been made with the aid of experimental techniques. Most experts believe that gene therapy for more general diseases will have a positive effect on the longevity of cohorts born after 2010. In 2050, these generations will only be 40 years old and in a life stage in which death rates are still very low. Thus, no strong effect on life expectancy at birth may be expected at that time. Of course, the health of older cohorts will also be improved through medical progress, but it may be expected that as in the past, this will be a very gradual process and reductions in mortality will not be very large in the next decades.

Mortality by most causes of death is set to fall, first of all for cardiovascular deaths. Most experts foresee advances in medical treatments and reductions in the risk factors related to coronary heart disease, such as smoking, diet and hypertension. A (further) decline in, for instance, stomach cancer is also expected. However, deaths caused by a number of other cancers, especially lung cancer among women, and deaths from suicide will continue to rise.

5.4 | Mortality Assumptions

5.4.1. Method of Projection Mortality

The key assumptions of the Uniformity and Diversity scenarios have been formulated on the basis of the cultural and economic determinants of mortality and of the prospects for the future discussed. The assumptions have been specified in both qualitative and quantitative terms. In translating the qualitative assumptions into quantitative assumptions, the 'Life expectancy at birth' was used as the main indicator of mortality. This measure can be derived from a life table with all age-specific mortality rates per calendar year as input.

The quantitative assumptions of the scenarios involve the specification of life expectancy in the two scenarios for each of the five clusters of countries.

In order to arrive at a specified life expectancy an age pattern of mortality rates has to be generated. This is done in both scenarios for each cluster. For the intermediate years between the last observation and the target year for each country an age-specific curvilinear path is used.

5.4.2. Uniformity Scenario

The Uniformity scenario assumes that over the next fifty years economic and cultural trends will converge, so that around 2050 an undivided Europe will stretch from the Atlantic Ocean to Siberia. Under this scenario, there will be no political, financial, social or cultural barriers and as a result prosperity will spread to all parts of Europe. Medical technology will make major advances and the financial situation will provide everybody with access to the growing medical facilities. Moreover, healthy lifestyles will gain ground and the environment (micro and macro) will be well protected or even improved. As economic conditions have a larger impact on men than on women, the growth of prosperity will cause a decline in gender differences in life expectancy. Finally, towards the middle of the 21st century mortality patterns will be the same across Europe.

In recent decades both male and female mortality have converged in the countries of northern, western and southern Europe. In addition, gender differences have decreased slightly. The general assumptions of the Uniformity scenario are in line with these trends. The average annual increase in life expectancy for northern, western and southern Europe is first set to follow the observed trend, but it will gradually become smaller during the course of the scenario period. The main reason for this is that mortality rates for young age groups are already low and only a limited further reduction may be expected. Reductions in mortality rates at older ages, even if these are of the same magnitude as in the past, will have a lesser impact on life expectancy. In general the survival curve will become more rectangular. This means that large proportions of people will survive to older ages, after which the survival curve drops sharply to zero.

In northern, western and southern Europe, life expectancy at birth has increased by an average of 0.2 years per calendar year since 1970. A continuation of this trend in the first half of the 21st century would imply that life expectancy would increase by more than ten years. Under the Uniformity scenario, future increases in life expectancy in countries in which levels are already relatively high, are set to slow down because it will become increasingly difficult to achieve further improvements in life expectancy at birth if mortality rates are already low. Therefore, in countries with current low levels of mortality, life expectancy at birth will increase by less than ten years until 2050. Since female life expectancy is already high in most countries of northern, western and southern Europe (around 80 years), the future increase will be smaller for women than for men. Around 2050, life expectancy at birth will be similar in all European countries: 83 years for men and 86 years for women (Table 5.1 and *Figures 5.2* and *5.3*).

Figure 5.2a. Mean life expectancy at birth, females

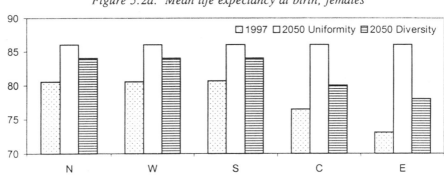

Figure 5.2b. Mean life expectancy at birth, males

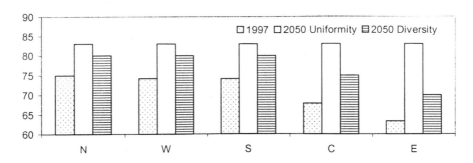

Figure 5.3. Sex difference in life expectancy at birth

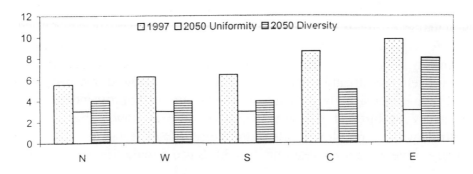

This implies that in central and eastern Europe, a strong increase in life expectancy is expected from the very start of the scenario period. In these countries favourable socioeconomic and cultural developments may have a strong and rather quick positive impact on survival. The fact that current life expectancy in northern, western and southern Europe is much higher than in central and eastern Europe implies that a strong increase in life expectancy in central and eastern Europe does not require a technical breakthrough. Under the Uniformity scenario, life expectancy in central and eastern Europe will therefore increase more strongly than the average past increase in the western part of Europe. In the central and eastern European countries the survival curve will also become more rectangular, albeit in the more distant future. The average increase in life expectancy in central and eastern Europe will therefore also gradually become smaller during the course of the 21st century.

Since female life expectancy is less dependent on the economic situation than male life expectancy, the favourable economic developments assumed in the Uniformity scenario are likely to have a stronger impact on male than on female life expectancy. Furthermore, lifestyle differences between men and women will also become smaller. Consequently, the gender gap will decrease to three years in 2050 (*Figure 5.4*).

5.4.3. Diversity Scenario

The Diversity scenario assumes that political, economic and social differences between the West and the East will persist. A partitioned Europe is the result. Under this scenario, economic prospects are gloomy. The economic situation is set to remain particularly poor in eastern Europe and foreign help will not suffice to solve the problems. Technological developments will be slow and the welfare situation will stay rather unfavourable. As a result, lifestyles, in particular male lifestyles, will also remain unhealthy. Moreover, environmental decay will not come to a halt. Some medical progress will be achieved, however (partly taken over from the West), and some social and medical programmes will be completed. The political and social chaos of the 1990s will be replaced by a more stable, albeit not perfect, governmental system. Life expectancy, in particular that of women, will increase slightly, although this will by no means allow these countries to catch up with levels found in northern,

Figure 5.4. Increase in life expectancy at birth

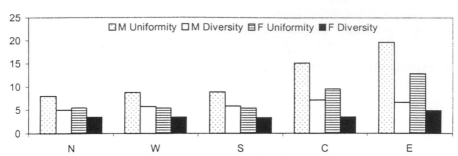

western and southern Europe. Developments in central Europe will lie somewhere between those found in the other two regions: better than in the East, worse than in the West.

In all regions, the increase in life expectancy at birth under the Diversity scenario will be smaller than under the Uniformity scenario. In northern, western and southern Europe the difference between both scenarios will be smaller than in central and eastern Europe. No differences among countries in northern, western, and southern Europe are imputed. Current differences in mortality across countries in these regions are expected to be temporary. Life expectancy in Portugal, which is currently relatively low, will follow a similarly favourable development to that observed in Greece, Italy and Spain in recent decades. While in northern, western and southern Europe life expectancy is set to increase to 80 years for men and 84 years for women, in central Europe life expectancy will increase to 75 years for men and 80 years for women, and in eastern Europe to 70 years for men and 78 years for women. In 2050 the gender difference in life expectancy under the Diversity scenario will range from four (in northern, western and southern Europe) to eight years (in eastern Europe).

5.4.4. *Differences between the scenarios: the age-specific mortality patterns of Sweden and Bulgaria*

In the mortality scenarios, assumptions are made on future changes in mortality rates by age and gender. Because a detailed description of these would require too much space, mortality will be described for two countries only, one belonging to a cluster with a high life expectancy

(Sweden) and one belonging to a cluster with a low life expectancy (Bulgaria). This choice has been prompted partly by the availability of observed age-specific mortality rates. As the socioeconomic conditions in these two countries are quite different, they can serve as an illustration of the variation in age-specific assumptions between both scenarios.

Figure 5.5 presents the age-specific mortality rates for 1995. The most striking difference between Sweden and Bulgaria is child mortality. The rates for Bulgaria at ages one to five are five times higher than those for Sweden. Beyond that age, the difference gradually becomes smaller. At the age of 20, the Bulgarian rates are about twice as high as the Swedish rates, for men slightly higher and for women somewhat lower. Around the age of 50, the Bulgarian rates are three times (males) and 1.5 times (females) as high as the Swedish rates. Around the age of 65, the factor is two for both sexes. Beyond that age the difference for males gradually decreases, but the difference for females remains rather constant.

Using the 1995 life table based on the mortality rates, the percentages of survivors can be calculated. At every age, Bulgarian males have the least number of survivors and Swedish females the most. The figures for Bulgarian females and Swedish males are about the same (*Figure 5.6*). Whereas at age 70 only slightly more than 50 per cent of Bulgarian men are still alive, more than 80 per cent of Swedish females survive to this age. Their numbers do not drop to 50 per cent until the age of 85.

Under the Uniformity scenario, differences in mortality between all countries and therefore also those between Bulgaria and Sweden disappear completely. This means that for Bulgaria, life expectancy will increase by 11 years for females and by 15 years for males (*Figure 5.7*). For Sweden, these figures are only 4.5 and 7.0 years. Death rates in Bulgaria must therefore decline particularly strongly (*Figure 5.8*). At many ages the assumed reduction is 80 per cent. For Sweden, the reduction, at 60 per cent, is also very high for many ages. It needs no saying that in the event of a larger increase in life expectancy than the increase assumed for Bulgaria, which is the case for all other countries in the eastern cluster, reductions in mortality rates need to be even stronger. For Bulgarian men, in particular, the median age of survival increases very strongly under the Uniformity scenario: from about 70 to almost 85 years (Figure 5.6). The median age for Bulgarian women increases by about ten years, to 88 years.

Figure 5.5a. Mortality rates of Bulgaria and Sweden, 1995, 1-39 years old

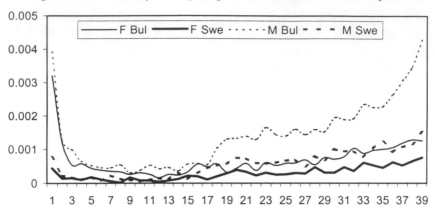

Figure 5.5b. Mortality rates of Bulgaria and Sweden, 1995, 40-64 years old

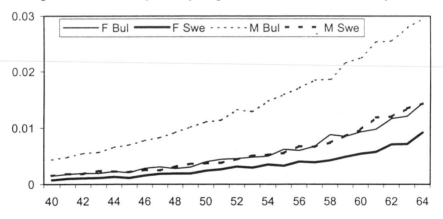

Figure 5.5c. Mortality rates of Bulgaria and Sweden, 1995, 65-94 years old

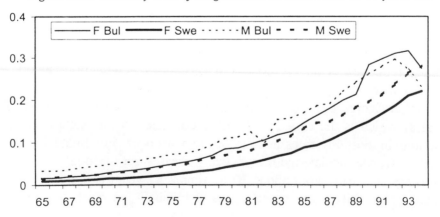

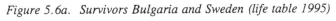

Figure 5.6a. Survivors Bulgaria and Sweden (life table 1995)

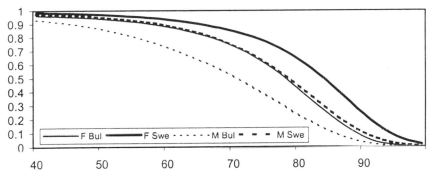

Figure 5.6b. Survivors in Uniformity scenario (life table 2050)

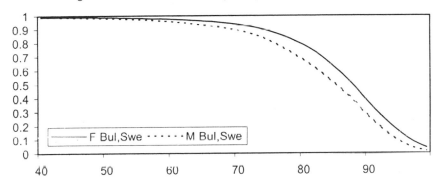

Figure 5.6c. Survivors in Diversity scenario (life table 2050)

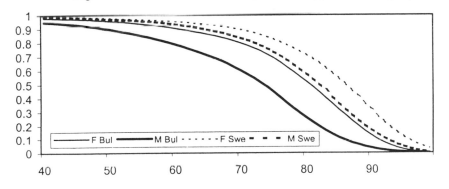

Figure 5.7. Life expectancy, 1985-2050, Bulgaria and Sweden

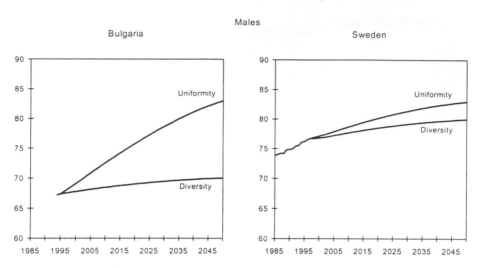

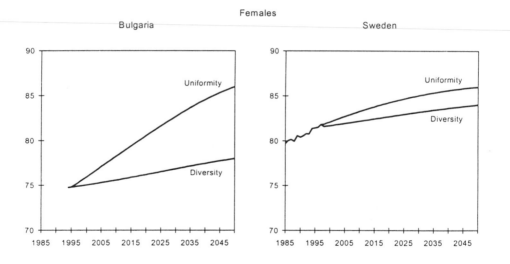

The median ages of survival in 2050 for Swedish men and women are also 85 and 88 years, respectively, and consequently smaller increases need to take place, since the median ages are currently 78 and 84 years.

Under the Diversity scenario life expectancies are set to increase much less. For Bulgaria, about three years for both men and women and for Sweden 2.5 years for women and four years for men. The reductions are

Figure 5.8. Mortality rates, Bulgaria and Sweden

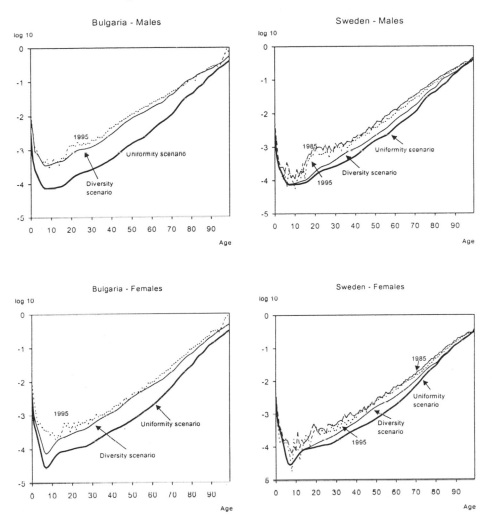

much smaller, but nevertheless about 25 per cent, for many ages in Bulgaria, and 30 to 40 per cent in Sweden. So, here too, a moderate increase in life expectancy can only be achieved if death rates decline considerably.

Of course, under the Diversity scenario the median ages of survival increase to a lesser extent than under the Uniformity scenario. For Bulgarian men, the median age increases from about 70 to about 74 years, for Bulgarian women from 78 to 81 years, for Swedish men from 78 to 82 and for Swedish women from 84 to 86 years.

6. Uniformity and Diversity Scenarios for International Migration

Nicole VAN DER GAAG and Leo VAN WISSEN

6.1 | Introduction

Although international migration has been included only recently as a separate component of population change in demographic projections, it has become one of its key elements (Salt and Singleton, 1995). In a growing number of countries, the migration component is now more important for population growth than natural increase (Münz, 1990), which has recently even become negative in some cases. For most European countries this is a new demographic situation. Until the 1970s, high fertility caused the well-known baby-boom in Europe, which, combined with reduced mortality levels, was the main component of population growth after the Second World War. It was also after the Second World War that Europe turned into an important immigration area. At first, the threat of an impenetrable Iron Curtain cutting off the states in central and eastern Europe from the rest of Europe, made many people flee to the west. Moreover, due to the process of de-colonisation many European countries with a colonial history have experienced substantial inflows of returning migrants. This process often resulted in permanent migratory contacts between the former colonies and the colonisers (Van de Kaa, 1996b). Furthermore, by the end of the 1950s and continuing into the 1960s migration to northwest Europe was generated by a growing demand for labour (Fassmann and Münz, 1992). These migrant workers came

J. de Beer and L. van Wissen (eds.),
European: One Continent, Different Worlds Population Scenarios for the 21st Century, 91–108.
© 1999 Kluwer Academic Publishers. Printed in the Netherlands.

primarily from southern European countries, from Turkey and later from northern Africa. The significance of labour migration declined as a result of the oil crisis in 1972/73, and migration for reasons of family reunification and family formation gained importance (King, 1993). Around the mid-1980s several traditional emigration countries in southern Europe developed into immigration countries. This was partially due to net inflows of their own returning nationals, and partly to the fact that they had become net receivers of citizens from northwest Europe and migrants from northern Africa (Salt *et al.*, 1994).

In central and eastern Europe the end of the communist era marked the beginning of fundamental changes in international migration patterns. International migration was virtually absent in this part of Europe during the communist era, not because its citizens did not want to move, but because the system prohibited the free movement of people. After the fall of the Iron Curtain, large migration flows emerged, making up for decades of migratory inertia. The central and eastern European countries are currently in a process of cultural, economic and social restructuring. This is reflected in large population movements driven by both ethnic and economic forces. The demographic effects of these societal transitions will most likely not be limited to the present, but will also extend into the future.

Despite its key role in population growth, migration is very difficult to project. The uncertainties surrounding migration forecasts are much larger than those of either mortality or fertility. Much more so than the other demographic components, migration depends on short-term developments and national policies, which may result in substantial differences in migration intensities from one year to another. In the period 1985-1997, for instance, international migration flows in Europe were very closely related to specific historical events. Events such as the reunification of Germany, the fall of the Iron Curtain and the war in former Yugoslavia triggered large migration flows within Europe. In response to these large migration flows into the more prosperous countries of predominantly northern and western Europe, immigration policies have become increasingly restrictive since the mid-1990s, resulting in considerable decreases in migration levels. Net migration to Germany, for instance, has recently more than halved. Due to these large differences in migration intensities, future developments are seldom continuations of past trends.

Therefore, extrapolation techniques are of limited value in forecasting international migration. The prospects for scenario analysis, on the other hand, are more promising (Willekens, 1992, Van de Kaa, 1993).

An additional problem in migration research is the lack of data on migration flows. Migration flow data are only available in countries with a migration register. In most other countries annual migration data are estimated from other sources or do not exist. As a result, in the compilation of the two scenarios flow data are not used. Instead, net migration was calculated as the age- and sex-specific balance between population change and natural growth in each year. This method implied that net migration should be interpreted as net migration plus net administrative corrections. Because this method was applied to all countries, international consistency was achieved and problems of missing data and incomparability of migration figures, resulting from, for instance, definition problems, do not apply.

6.2 | Backgrounds to Differences in International Migration Trends in Europe

6.2.1. Northern Europe

In the period 1985-1996, most countries in the Nordic cluster saw a rapid rise in immigration due to huge flows of refugees and asylum seekers, originating mostly from former Yugoslavia. On average, annual net in-flows of migrants are in the order of one to three per thousand inhabitants. The inflow reached its peak in 1987 in Norway and in 1994 in Sweden. Following the introduction of a visa regime for Bosnians and some other nationals of former Yugoslavia in most northern countries, asylum flows from this region have fallen considerably in recent years.

In Denmark, Norway and Sweden, in particular, nationals of other Nordic countries also accounted for a substantial part of the net inflows. This is not surprising, however, as in general there are relatively few barriers for nationals of Nordic countries to move to another country in the region. The position of other Nordic nationals in the labour market, for example, is more or less comparable to that of national workers (in Denmark), or at least considerably better than that of foreigners from non-Nordic countries. Immigration into Finland between 1989 and 1991 rose sharply, not only as a result of increasing numbers of refugees and asylum seekers, but also due to the return of ethnic Finns from Russia and Estonia. Russian citizens constitute the second largest group of immigrants in Finland, after ethnic Finns. Although principal destinations for Icelanders moving abroad are Denmark, Norway and Sweden, Iceland may be considered an outsider within the Nordic cluster because it is traditionally a country of net emigration. In recent years, however, immigration to Iceland for reasons of work has become increasingly prominent.

6.2.2. *Western Europe*

Within Europe, the relationship between economic developments and international migration seems to be most apparent in the western European countries. For several countries, the connection between unemployment and gross immigration is demonstrated by King (1993). This relationship, however, has been disturbed by policy interventions. As in northern Europe, in the west, too, the growing number of asylum seekers has been one of the most important developments in international migration patterns in the late 1980s and early 1990s (Kupiszewski, 1996). On average, net migration per thousand inhabitants rose from about one in 1985 to a peak of almost five in 1992, after which a major decline in net migration was observed, falling to two in 1996. For most countries, 1993 marked a turning point. Due to more restrictive immigration policies, net inflows levelled off (Belgium, Luxembourg, United Kingdom), decreased, or even dropped sharply (Austria, Germany, Switzerland).

The highest net migration levels were found in Luxembourg, Germany, Switzerland and Austria, while a negative migration balance was found in Ireland. In recent years, however, Ireland has turned into a net receiver of migrants, mainly due to returning Irish nationals, who are attracted by the booming Irish economy. For the same reason the numbers of emigrants are declining. The migration balance in Switzerland, on the other hand, has recently changed into slightly negative values. This seems to be connected to the economic recession in the mid-1990s.

Large immigration flows into western Europe originate, besides from other European countries, from Africa and Asia. There are substantial differences in composition of migrant flows between countries, reflecting both geographical proximity as well as former colonial ties between the sending and receiving countries. For instance, immigration into the UK is dominated by Indians and Pakistanis, whereas French immigration originates mainly from Algeria and other former French colonies in Africa. German immigration largely originates from the relatively close central and eastern European countries, and includes many ethnic Germans ('Aussiedler'). In addition, although labour migration from Turkey and Morocco into western Europe has come to a halt, immigration from these countries for reasons of family reunion and family formation has become increasingly important. Migrants in Luxembourg are almost exclusively Europeans, the Portuguese accounting for the largest numbers. Although detailed data are lacking, immigration into Ireland is predominantly return migration from England and North America. Unfortunately, detailed data are also lacking for Austria and France. For Austria, comprehensive migration statistics were not compiled until recently, the first year of reporting being 1996 (Council of Europe, 1998).

6.2.3. Southern Europe

International migration patterns in the countries of southern Europe have changed completely over the last two decades: from being traditionally emigration countries they have become net receivers of migrants. This trend is visible in all four southern countries. The overall migration pattern in the south changed from slightly negative values into positive levels, with a maximum of well above two migrants per thousand of the total population in 1993. Italy and Spain, having by far the most sizeable populations in the southern cluster, largely shape the cluster's migration pattern. In Greece, net migration levels were substantially higher than the average, while in Portugal significantly lower levels were observed.

Two factors were primarily responsible for the transition from being an emigration into an immigration region: return migration of their own nationals and the arrival of increasing numbers of people from Africa, Asia and Latin America (Penninx, 1986). As the administrative structures in the south were not sufficiently prepared to deal with this new phenomenon, large inflows of migrants were allowed to settle undocumented. It took several years before legislative and administrative steps were taken to control illegal immigration. For this reason, it is very difficult to properly assess the magnitude of net migration in the south (Montanari and Cortese, 1993). Nevertheless, some remarks can be made about the origin of net immigration into the southern countries. Contrary to most other European countries, Italy is not a high net receiver of European migrants. This low balance is mainly caused by a relatively high net emigration to western Europe. Furthermore, a high positive migration balance may be observed with countries in Africa, followed by Asia and South America. The political turmoil on the other side of the Adriatic Sea has recently triggered large inflows of illegals from Albania into Italy. Contrary to the large numbers of illegal migrants, the number of asylum seekers in the southern countries is relatively low compared with western and northern Europe. Spain and Greece have relatively high net immigration flows from the countries of western Europe, among which a substantial number of return migrants. Portugal has a relatively high level of emigration to western and northern Europe.

6.2.4. Central and Eastern Europe

Before the collapse of the communist system, international migration into and out of the countries of central and eastern Europe was small compared with present-day figures. Out-migration from the USSR was almost non-existent before the 'perestroika', the only exception being Jewish out-migration. Between 1976 and 1986, an average of just under 25 000 Jews per year were allowed to leave the Soviet Union to Israel. Due to the fall of the Iron Curtain and the decreasing birth rates and increasing death rates, the significance of migration for population dynamics had risen sharply by the end of the 1980s. Between 1987 and 1990 outflows to non-USSR countries more or less doubled every year.

Present-day migration between the countries of central and eastern Europe is largely determined by ethnic flows of people returning to their home-lands (Council of Europe, 1998; Kupiszewski, 1996; Öberg and Boubnova, 1993). The inhabitants of central and eastern Europe belong to a variety of ethnic groups. Russians constitute the major group. As a result of Russian supremacy since the Second World War, millions of Russians settled in non-Russian parts of eastern Europe. Following the fall of the Iron Curtain, their presence in these now independent countries is being questioned, and the repatriation of Russian citizens from the former USSR republics has been set in motion. At the same time, ethnic minorities in Russia, such as the Baltic groups, have started to return to their homelands. Among these minorities are the 'Aussiedler' returning to Germany, pre-dominantly from Poland, the former Soviet Union and Romania (Van de Kaa, 1996b). In addition to ethnic migration, economic imbalances between eastern and western Europe are also giving rise to sizeable migration flows. In principle, capital moves to the east, where salaries are low, and labour moves to the west, where salaries are high (Öberg and Boubnova, 1993).

As a result of these developments, different international migration patterns can be observed in central European countries. In recent history, overall net migration was slightly negative, around minus one per thousand of the total population. Identical developments were observed in Estonia, Latvia and Lithuania. In these Baltic States, the migration balance was initially positive, but during the second half of the 1980s it started declining, until it eventually dropped below zero. From 1992 onwards, high levels of net emigration were observed, caused mainly by returning Russians, resulting in values of minus ten per thousand and below. After 1992, the negative migration balance was considerably reduced but it did not turn into positive values. In Poland, the Czech Republic and the Slovak Republic, on the other hand, immigration and emigration were more or less in equilibrium. Overall net migration to the east was positive in the late 1980s and early 1990s, at levels of one to two per thousand inhabitants. This was due primarily to the repatriation of Russians. Within the eastern region sizeable flows of repatriating Russians dominate the intra-cluster migration flows. While net migration to Russia has been positive in the last decade, in most of the other countries in eastern Europe net migration was negative during at least some years within this period.

6.3 | Migration Prospects for Europe

Looking at future migration developments in Europe, some general re-marks can be made. Firstly, in the coming years the economic gap between Europe and the developing world is not likely to be reduced to such an extent that the migration pressure from outside Europe will diminish (De Jong and Visser, 1997; Fassmann and Münz, 1992; Van de Kaa, 1996b). Consequently, the distribution of migration flows from the developing countries across Europe will be determined more by developments within Europe than by developments within the sending countries. Secondly, although some structural changes may take place in migration from eastern Europe to the west, such as a reduction in the number of asylum seekers from central and eastern European countries, the overall level of migration from the east to the west will probably remain high for a long time yet, due to the transitional nature of the central and eastern European economies (Fassmann and Münz, 1992; Kupiszewski, 1996). Thirdly, discussions about future migration patterns should increasingly be tied to the demographic process of ageing. Due to the very low fertility levels of recent decades, several European countries will face a declining working-age population in the decades ahead, which may lead to shortages in the labour market. In addition to other measures aimed at anticipating this phenomenon, such as stimulating (female) labour participation rates, the postponement of retirement and technological innovations, migration may also play a role in reducing these shortages (King, 1993). Bearing these general prospects in mind, two variants of international migration assumptions have been formulated.

6.4 | Migration Scenarios

6.4.1. Method

Quantitative migration assumptions are stated in terms of net migration per thousand of the total population. Although a breakdown of net migration into immigration and emigration flows is preferable for both methodological and theoretical reasons, this has not be done due to data limitations for a substantial number of countries. Instead, net migration was calculated as the age- and sex-specific balance between population change and natural growth in each year.

Under the Uniformity scenario, two different phases were specified, so that the time trend in the scenario period can be broken down into two separate profiles. For example, an increase in the first period may be followed by a flattening out of the trend or even a decrease in the second period. Moreover, the duration of the first phase differs across countries. The turning point in migration in the countries of central and eastern Europe will depend on the timing of their assumed entry into the European Union. For the countries that have already started formal negotiations, entry is assumed to take place before 2005. This applies to Estonia, Poland, the Czech Republic, Hungary and Slovenia. The second group of countries, Latvia, Lithuania, the Slovak Republic, Romania and Bulgaria, have not yet formally entered into negotiations, but they are likely to do so soon. For these countries, entry into the EU is expected to take place in 2010 at the latest. The remaining central and eastern countries are expected to join the EU somewhere in the period 2010-2020. For the countries of the northern, western and southern clusters, the first turning point will be reached in 2025, at least five years after all other European countries will have joined the European Union. Although Iceland, Norway and Switzerland are not members of the EU, the socioeconomic, cultural and demographic patterns in these countries are almost identical to those of the EU member states. Therefore, patterns similar to those of the EU are assumed for these three countries. Norway and Iceland are expected to follow the migration pattern of the north, whereas Switzerland is more likely to follow the pattern of the west. Furthermore, entry of Iceland, Norway and Switzerland into the EU is expected to take place anywhere between now and the end of the projection period without major implications for migration. For all countries, after the first turning point an assumed final target value of net migration rates will be reached in the year 2050. For the intermediate years a curvilinear path is assumed. Three different age- and sex-specific profiles of net migration were assumed: a northern, western and southern pattern (see *Figure 6.1*). These patterns are based on the international migration assumptions of the 1996 Eurostat national population scenarios (De Jong and Visser, 1997). Since no age-specific data were available for central and eastern Europe, these clusters were assumed to follow the age pattern of the northern cluster. Furthermore, the age pattern was kept constant during the entire projection period.

Under the Uniformity scenario, different migration trends are initially expected for each cluster. Within each cluster, migration patterns will converge to the first target level. In the second time interval of the projection period, the different cluster patterns are assumed to converge to the same target level in 2050, with the exception of southern Europe for which net

Figure 6.1. Net migration age profiles

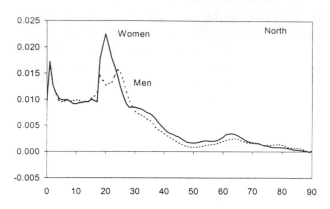

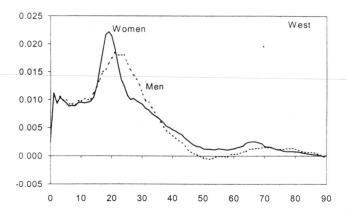

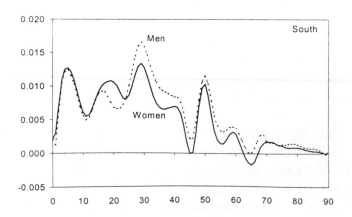

migration is expected to be somewhat higher than in the other clusters (see below).

Whereas under the Uniformity scenario, the time path towards one common rich and prosperous Europe is different for each cluster, under the Diversity scenario socioeconomic and cultural trends will not converge and existing differences will persist between central and eastern Europe on the one hand, and the European Union clusters on the other. Therefore, no dramatic changes are expected compared with current developments, and international migration under the Diversity scenario is assumed to follow a slow monotonic development over time. Only one target year (2050) is specified for all clusters. *Table 6.1* summarises the net migration assumptions used in both scenarios.

6.4.2. *Uniformity Scenario*

Under the Uniformity scenario, similar socioeconomic and cultural developments in 2050 are assumed for all European countries. Given that all countries will perform equally well at the end of the projection period, net migration within Europe for economic reasons is set to disappear. At the same time, however, cultural barriers to changing residence within Europe will be removed, resulting in increasing intra-European migration flows. We expect that cultural barriers will disappear before economic equality is reached. Consequently, migration will initially flow from economic poor countries in central and eastern Europe to the more prosperous countries in the north, west and south. Only after central and eastern European countries will have joined the EU, will these flows cease and will migration patterns in these countries develop along the same lines as those in the current EU countries. By the end of the projection period, in 2050, only marginal differences in the socioeconomic and cultural climate of all European countries will exist. By that time, the EU will have developed into a 'post-modern United States of Europe' in which all countries are equally attractive to live and work in. International barriers have been removed in the labour and housing markets. Due to the increased mobility (generated by greater opportunities), the level of intra-European migration will be high. As the various countries will be equally attractive, in- and out-migration into and from each country to other European countries will be more or less in equilibrium and consequently

Table 6.1. Net migration per thousand of the total population

	Base year 1996*	Uniformity			Diversity
		Target level 1	Reached in year	Final target level in 2050	Final target level in 2050
Denmark	3	3.5	2025	2.5	1.5
Finland	1	3.5	2025	2.5	1.5
Iceland	-2	3.5	2025	2.5	1.5
Norway	2	3.5	2025	2.5	1.5
Sweden	1	3.5	2025	2.5	1.5
Austria	1	3.5	2025	2.5	1.5
Belgium	1	3.5	2025	2.5	1.5
France	1	3.5	2025	2.5	1.5
Germany	3	3.5	2025	2.5	1.5
Ireland	1	3.5	2025	2.5	1.5
Luxembourg	9	3.5	2025	2.5	1.5
Netherlands	2	3.5	2025	2.5	1.5
Switzerland	1	3.5	2025	2.5	1.5
United Kingdom	2	3.5	2025	2.5	1.5
Greece	2	3.5	2025	3.5	2.5
Italy	2	3.5	2025	3.5	2.5
Portugal	1	3.5	2025	3.5	2.5
Spain	1	3.5	2025	3.5	2.5
Croatia	-3	-0.5	2020	2.5	-0.5
Czech Republic	1	-0.5	2005	2.5	-0.5
Estonia	-3	-0.5	2005	2.5	-0.5
Hungary	0	-0.5	2005	2.5	-0.5
Latvia	-3	-0.5	2010	2.5	-0.5
Lithuania	0	-0.5	2010	2.5	-0.5
Poland	0	-0.5	2005	2.5	-0.5
Slovak Republic	0	-0.5	2010	2.5	-0.5
Slovenia	1	-0.5	2005	2.5	-0.5
Belarus	1	-1	2020	2.5	-1
Bulgaria	0	-1	2010	2.5	-1
Moldavia	-3	-1	2020	2.5	-1
Romania	-1	-1	2010	2.5	-1
Russia	2	-1	2020	2.5	-1
Ukraine	-2	-1	2020	2.5	-1

* Base year 1996 with the exception of Croatia (1994), Moldavia, Russia, and Ukraine (1995). In a number of countries extreme observations were adjusted.

net intra-European migration will be low. The attitude towards non-European immigrants will be open-minded and immigration policies will be flexible. Anticipating an ultimately declining labour force due to ageing, and an increase in employment due to favourable socioeconomic developments, shortages in the labour market will be a real risk that countries will need to face. Although these shortages can not be compensated for by migration (the level of migration would have to be excessively high, as shown, for instance, by De Beer, 1996, and the European Commission, 1996), migration policies will make it relatively easy to recruit workers from outside Europe. As all countries are assumed to be equally attractive, a proportional distribution of inter-European migrants across all European countries is foreseen.

In the end, net migration developments are expected to be similar in all clusters, with one exception. In a situation where socioeconomic and cultural developments are assumed to be more or less similar among countries, the only remaining dimension leading to differences in migration patterns is climatic and geographical attractiveness. The many different ways of living in Europe, expressed, for example in different life styles and in consumption patterns are not confined to specific countries but are spread across different population groups. People can adapt their behaviour, and products can be exported. Climatic and geographic characteristics, on the other hand, are fixed and unique for each country. To enjoy these specific amenities of a country, people need to move to the regions in question. For this reason, even under the Uniformity scenario lasting differences in migration are to be expected. Due to the highly attractive climatic and geographical environment of southern Europe, net migration to this cluster is expected to be somewhat higher than migration to the other clusters. It is assumed that the favourable geographical location of southern Europe will be particularly attractive to elderly migrants. The relatively high inflow of mostly wealthy, elderly people will increase employment, which may in turn trigger flows of labour migration, and thus of young people. As a result, southern Europe will clearly benefit from this inflow. The additional stimulus provided by this group of migrants to this region will in turn attract new industrial activities, resulting in an upward economic development, which in turn will boost labour migration. Net migration will therefore increase, not only among the elderly, but also among younger age groups. Similar developments have taken place in the

United States in recent decades, where the 'Sunbelt' states of Florida and California have benefited from their natural amenities in this manner.

6.4.3. Diversity Scenario

Compared with the Uniformity scenario, less favourable socioeconomic developments are assumed under the Diversity scenario. Economic differences among the countries of the EU (as well as Norway, Iceland and Switzerland) will disappear, but differences among these EU clusters on the one hand and the central and eastern European clusters on the other will grow. Due to the relatively unfavourable economic developments, the demand for workers from outside Europe will be small, resulting in stricter attitudes towards immigration. Moreover, since cultural differences will persist, cultural barriers to migration will remain as well, making it even more difficult for migrants to enter the Union. At the same time, however, increased economic differences between the EU clusters and central and eastern Europe will heighten migration pressure from central and eastern Europe to the EU. Migrants will certainly try to seize any opportunities that come their way in the economically more prosperous countries. As a result of these developments, migration policies in the EU clusters will become even more restrictive, turning the EU into a 'Fortress Europe'. Under the Diversity scenario, the level of inter- and intra-European migration flows will therefore be substantially lower than under the Uniformity scenario.

Under the Diversity scenario, migration is not only smaller in size, but also highly selective (the so-called 'brain drain'). In the EU clusters, preference will be given to the often highly educated and culturally more similar migrants from central and eastern Europe over migrants from other continents. Central Europe, in turn, and to a lesser extent eastern Europe, will be attractive destinations for migrants from the rest of the world who enter these countries with the intention of moving on to the EU (transit migration). Because of the unfavourable economic circumstances in central and eastern Europe, the outflow to the EU clusters will not be completely offset by the inflow from outside Europe, resulting ultimately in a negative migration balance. Net migration in the countries of the EU clusters will remain positive during the entire projection period. As under the Uniformity scenario, the south will develop relatively more favourably than the other clusters. Due to a high level of ageing, the need for labour will be relative-ly large in the south, irrespective of socioeconomic and cultural develop-ments. This economic boom will not, however, occur before the end of the projection period.

6.4.4. Main Differences between the Uniformity and the Diversity Scenario

The results of the different migration assumptions in terms of absolute numbers of migrants differ across the clusters. In the northern and western clusters similar patterns will be observed in all countries. Net migration figures are higher under the Uniformity scenario than under the Diversity scenario for the entire projection period. Under the Uniformity scenario, in all countries but Luxembourg absolute numbers of migrants will increase until the year 2025 after which a slight decline will set in. Since under this scenario all European countries will have entered the European Union by 2020 at the latest, the countries of the north and the west will start losing their favoured position, resulting in slightly declining migration levels.

Under the Diversity scenario, only marginal changes in migration numbers will be observed in most countries until the end of the projection period (see, for example, the pattern for Sweden in *Figure 6.2*). The pattern for Luxembourg is somewhat different, as net migration to Luxembourg is rather high (on average nine per thousand inhabitants in the period 1985-1997) and it is unlikely that net migration to this country will remain at the current high level for many years to come. Under both the Uniformity and the Diversity scenarios, a significant decline in net migration numbers is expected for the first two to three decades, followed by more or less stable numbers until the mid 21st century (see *Figure 6.3*).

In the southern cluster, net migration under the Uniformity scenario also exceeds the corresponding number under the Diversity scenario during the entire period. Since, according to the Uniformity scenario, the southern European countries will develop most positively compared with the other clusters, the relatively high net immigration reached around 2025 will continue until the end of the projection period. Under the Diversity scenario, on the other hand, net immigration will be more or less stable or will level off after an initial small increase (*Figure 6.4* gives the pattern for Italy). Since net migration per thousand is assumed to be constant in the

Nicole van der Gaag and Leo van Wissen

Figure 6.2. Net migration in Sweden

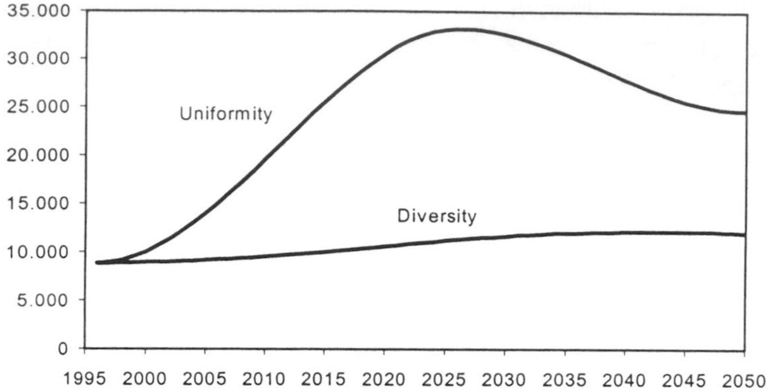

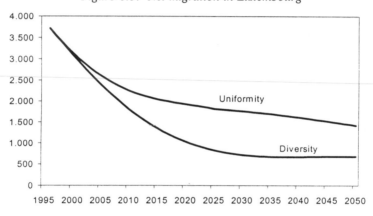

Figure 6.3. Net migration in Luxembourg

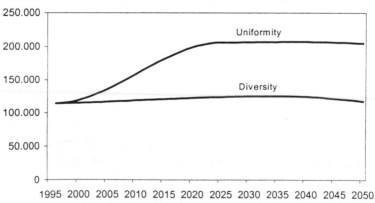

Figure 6.4. Net migration in Italy

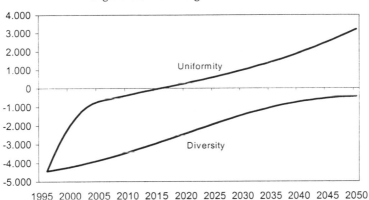

Figure 6.5. Net migration in Estonia

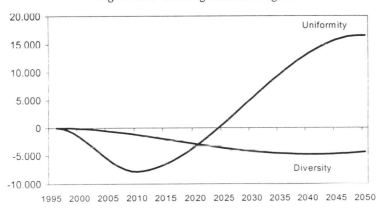

Figure 6.6. Net migration in Bulgaria

period 2025-2050, this slightly declining trend may be attributed to a declining population as a result of natural decrease.

Depending on the migration level in the base year of the projection period, two different migration patterns will be observed in central and eastern Europe. In Croatia, Latvia, Estonia, Moldavia, Romania and Ukraine net migration under the Diversity scenario is expected to be negative over the entire period. As recently observed migration levels for these countries are highly negative, the migration balance is set to become somewhat less negative in the future. Under the Uniformity scenario, net migration will increase strongly and will turn into positive values in around ten to fifteen years' time, after these countries have joined the European Union (see, for example, the pattern for Estonia in *Figure 6.5*). For these countries, it is argued that the relatively high net emigration numbers of today will not continue into the future. The necessity to move out of the country will disappear as the socioeconomic situation improves. Moreover, many emigrants from central and eastern European countries are ethnic Russians who are returning to Russia. The large numbers of repatriating Russians cannot continue at this level in the future because, eventually, most of them will have returned. These flows will thus dry up. In the remaining countries of central and eastern Europe, net migration today is zero or positive. These countries will therefore face continually declining migration numbers under the Diversity scenario, reaching negative values during the course of the projection period. In contrast, under the Uniformity scenario net migration will initially drop even stronger, resulting in lower numbers of migrants under the Uniformity scenario than under the Diversity scenario at the beginning of the projection period. After some time, however, when their economies catch up with those of the EU countries, net migration will increase strongly, resulting ultimately in significant differences in net numbers of migrants between the two scenarios (see, for instance, the pattern for Bulgaria in *Figure 6.6*). The higher net migration at the beginning of the projection period under the Diversity scenario compared with the Uniformity scenario can be explained by the enhanced possibilities of moving into the EU clusters under the latter scenario. As under the Diversity scenario, it will be difficult for *all* migrants to move to the EU, emigration flows from central and eastern Europe to the EU will diminish, and transit migrants from outside Europe travelling via central and eastern Europe to the European Union, will be prevented from entering the Union, resulting initially in higher net migration flows in the central and eastern clusters under the Diversity scenario compared with the Uniformity scenario.

7. Population Development in Europe in the 21st Century

Wim VAN HOORN, Nicole VAN DER GAAG and Corina HUISMAN

7.1 | Introduction

As described for each demographic component separately in the previous chapters of this volume, demographic trends in Europe have changed significantly in the last decades of the 20th century. In the countries of the European Economic Area (EEA) plus Switzerland, declining fertility levels and extended life expectancies have altered the age distribution of the population. The general trend is one of ageing: a declining percentage of young people combined with a major increase in the percentage of elderly. The countries of central and eastern Europe experienced rapid demographic changes after 1990, due to the radical political, economic and social changes which followed the collapse of the Communist system. In these countries, fertility has dropped considerably over the past decade while at the same time most of these countries experienced a decline in life expectancy, resulting in significantly lower values compared to the countries of the EEA. Another new demographic development of the second half of the 20th century is that Europe, once an emigration continent, has turned into a major immigration region. Immigration is mainly directed towards the economically more prosperous countries of the EEA, whereas several central and eastern European countries face zero or negative net migration numbers.

An important question is whether (and if so, how) today's demographic situation in Europe will change during the first decades of the 21st century. In this volume the question is phrased in a slightly different manner: will

J. de Beer and L. van Wissen (eds.),
European: One Continent, Different Worlds Population Scenarios for the 21st Century, 109–147.

demographic differences between countries decline as a result of economic
and cultural trends, or will differences persist or even increase? To answer
this question, two population scenarios have been compiled in the previous
chapters, each one pertaining to one of the two contrasting answers to this
question. The Uniformity scenario assumes that economic and cultural trends,
and thus, trends in fertility, mortality, and migration will converge in the long
run and consequently that differences across countries will decline; in contrast,
the Diversity scenario assumes that both economic and cultural differences
will persist or even increase and that demographic differences across countries
will remain.

This chapter presents the main outcomes of the two population scenarios. The
focus will be on demographic developments in Europe as a whole, as well as
in five clusters of countries which were introduced in Chapter 3 (the northern
or Maternalistic cluster, the western or Pragmatic cluster, the southern or
Paternalistic cluster, the central or Intermediate cluster and the eastern or Post-
totalitarian cluster). Only limited attention will be paid to developments in
individual countries. Several topics will be discussed, among which total
population change, the influence of natural growth versus net migration,
ageing, dejuvenation and expected developments in the working-age
population. In the next sections we will first present the results by topic. Major
differences between both scenarios are highlighted for all clusters. We will
then give a short summary of the results by cluster. Appendix 1 contains more
detailed scenario results by country and cluster.

7.2 | Population Change

In 1996 the population of the 33 countries of Europe included in this study
totalled 707 million people. The vast majority lived in western and eastern
Europe. The most populous country is Russia (147 million inhabitants),
followed by Germany (82 million), the United Kingdom, France and Italy
(around 58 million people each). Luxembourg and Iceland, on the other hand,
have the smallest populations (0.4 and 0.3 million people, respectively).

Under the Uniformity scenario, political and cultural barriers will disappear
and the economy will flourish all over Europe. As a result, in the long run,
fertility, life expectancy at birth and net international migration will be
comparatively high. According to this scenario total population will grow to

733 million in 2050. This implies a growth of almost four per cent. A peak in the growth rate will be reached around 2020, when the population will increase by almost one million people each year. Thereafter, annual growth will decline continuously and after 2047 population growth will become slightly negative.

Population growth is not equally distributed across Europe. Initial differences in mortality and fertility plus differences in the age structures of the various populations are the main causes of differences in trends among different countries or clusters. In fact, growth will take place only in the northern, western and southern parts of Europe. In these regions population growth varies from five per cent in the south (from 117 to 123 million people) to 18 per cent in the north and the west (from 24 to 28 million and from 244 to 286 million people, respectively, *Figure 7.1* and *7.2*). Growth in these regions is expected to be particularly strong around 2025 (*Figure 7.3*). Despite the growth expectations present in this scenario, the size of the population in central Europe is not set to change very much. After 2020 a slight decrease is expected (from 79 to 77 million people). The population trend in eastern Europe is even negative. In this region, despite significant increases in fertility and life expectancy under the Uniformity scenario, the population will decline continuously from 244 to 218 million people, corresponding to an 11 per cent fall. The initially very low levels of fertility and life expectancy as well as the present age structure appear to have a long-lasting effect on future demographic trends in these regions.

As far as individual countries are concerned, the strongest growth is expected for the smallest countries in northern and western Europe. Of the countries with more than 30 million inhabitants, only France and the United Kingdom are expected to grow by more than 15 per cent (*Figure 7.4*). Not surprisingly, given the developments of the clusters as a whole, a population decline is expected for most of the central and eastern European countries. Only Poland, the Slovak Republic and Moldavia are expected to show a slight increase of three to five per cent.

Under the Diversity scenario, economic and socio-cultural barriers in Europe will persist and large differences in fertility, life expectancy and international migration will remain. For all demographic components, lower values are assumed than under the Uniformity scenario and this has a marked negative effect on total population growth. The European population will decrease

Figure 7.1. Population, 1996-2050

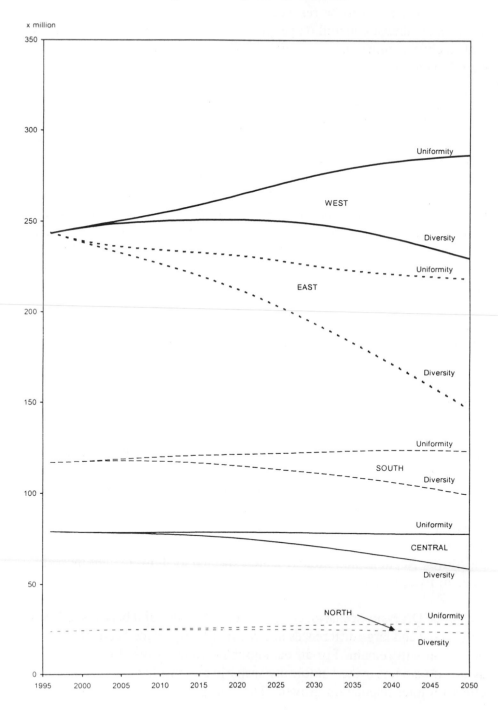

Figure 7.2. Population (1996=100)

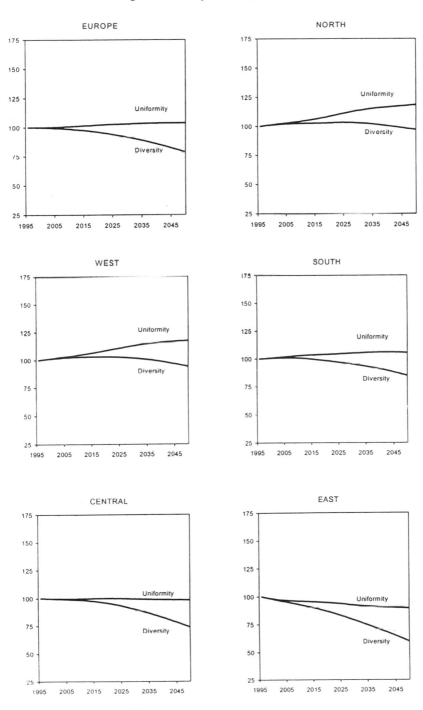

Figure 7.3. Population growth, 1996-2050

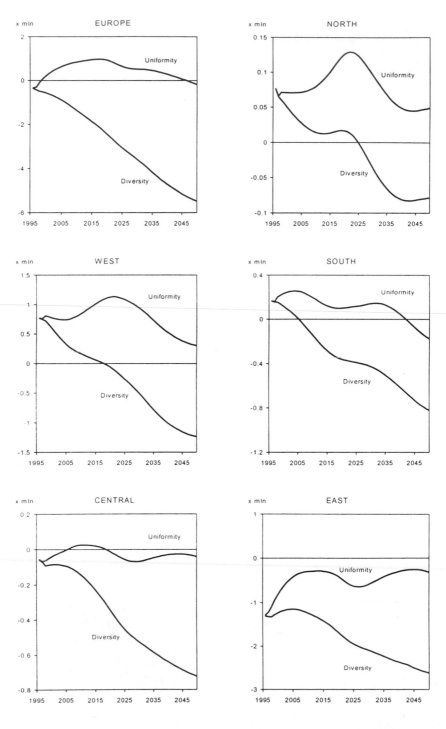

substantially: from 707 million in 1996 to 557 million in 2050, a decline by about 20 per cent (Figures 7.1 to 7.3). Whereas the total European population is currently decreasing by less than 0.5 million a year, under the Diversity scenario the annual 'loss' will be over five million by 2050. This development is accounted for mainly by eastern and central Europe, where the population will decrease by as much as 40 per cent (from 244 to 146 million) and by 26 per cent (from 79 to 58 million), respectively. In the Mediterranean region, in the period until 2050 the decline will be roughly 15 per cent (from 117 to 99 million). In the northern and western regions, the population size will not decrease until about 2020 and by 2050 the population will be only about five per cent smaller than today (a decline from 24 to 23 million people in the north and from 244 to 230 million people in the west).

Looking at individual countries, the most striking result is that the populations of Bulgaria, Ukraine and Latvia will be almost halved by 2050. For about half of the countries the population is expected to decline by at least 15 per cent. An increase is expected for only five countries (Denmark, Iceland, Norway, Ireland and Luxembourg, *Figure 7.5*).

7.3 | Natural Growth versus Net Migration

Population change is the combined result of natural growth (the number of births minus the number of deaths) and net migration. Although natural growth in Europe has traditionally been positive, this is not likely to continue in the future. Even under the Uniformity scenario, where fertility and life expectancy at birth will be comparatively high, natural growth is expected to be negative for the entire period 1996-2050, which reflects the overriding effect of the aged population structure in Europe. The large positive migration balance of Europe, with migrants arriving from other regions in the world, accounts for a continuous population increase until 2047 under this scenario (*Figure 7.6*).

Developments in natural growth in the five clusters differ strongly. On the one hand, in the northern and western parts of Europe, natural growth today is still above one per thousand inhabitants and is, according to the Uniformity scenario, only expected to fall slowly in the next decade. Thereafter, a slight increase is expected until around 2020. However, the number of deaths is not expected to exceed the number of births before the 2030s. In southern Europe, on the other hand, the situation is quite different. Here, natural growth is

Figure 7.4. Population in Europe 2050 (1996=100)
Uniformity

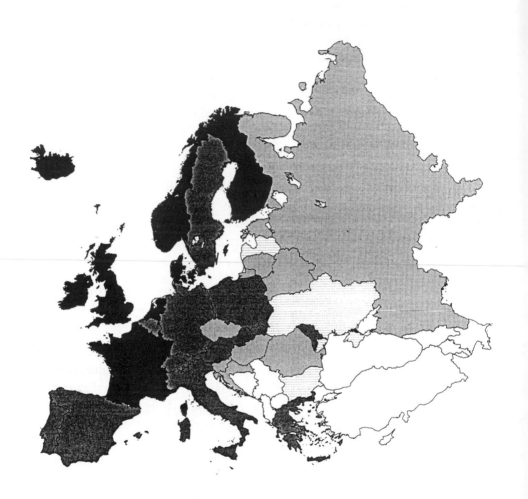

■ 115 or more (9)
▨ 100 to 115 (12)
▦ 85 to 100   (9)
□ less than 85 (3)

Figure 7.5. Population in Europe 2050 (1996=100)
Diversity

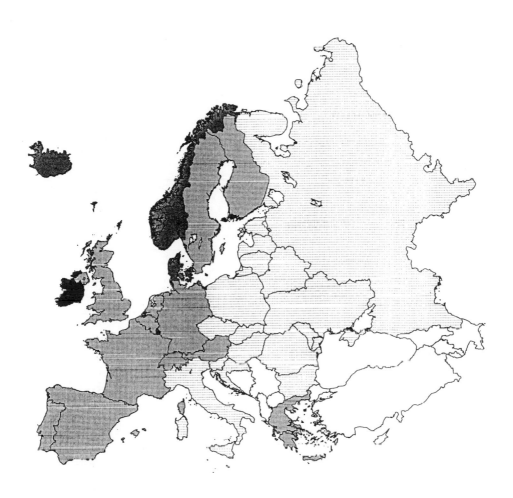

■ 115 or more (1)
■ 100 to 115   (4)
▨ 85 to 100   (12)
☐ less than 85 (16)

Figure 7.6. Net migration and natural increase, 1996-2050

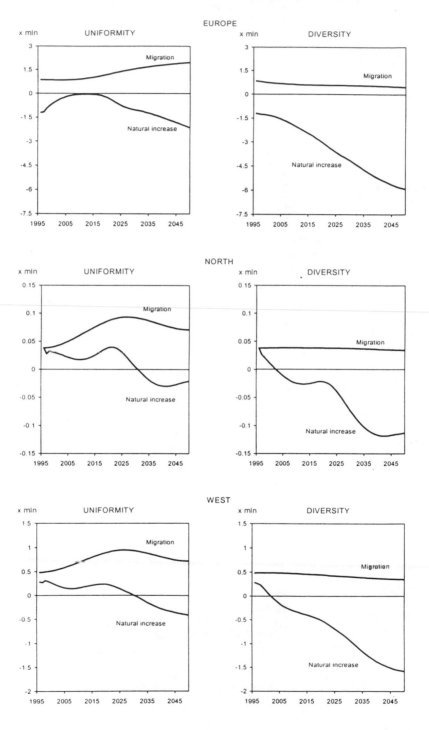

Figure 7.6. Net migration and natural increase, 1996-2050 (end)

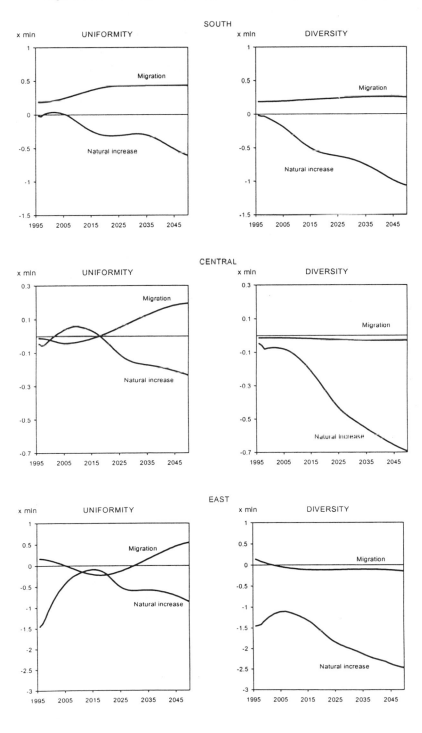

already very low or even negative, and population growth is almost completely due to high positive net migration levels. Under the Uniformity scenario, natural growth is set to reach negative values before 2015 in all countries of southern Europe. Another consequence of low fertility levels in this region at present and in the recent past is that ageing has already progressed relatively strongly compared with the other regions and the resulting demographic pattern is one of a small number of births and a continuously growing number of deaths. After 2040, negative natural growth will be stronger than positive net migration, which means that the population will start to decline.

In the eastern region, natural growth is fairly negative today (minus six per thousand) and the slightly positive migration balance does not compensate for this component. The current situation is mainly caused by low fertility levels and relatively high mortality rates. Under the Uniformity scenario, the current gloomy demographic situation is expected to improve soon, resulting in strongly diminishing population losses due to increasing natural growth. Positive values, however, will never be reached. Due to ageing, natural growth will decrease again after 2015 from minus 0.4 per thousand to minus 4.0 per thousand in 2050. The pattern of net migration to eastern Europe is the opposite of the pattern of natural growth, albeit at a lower level: a small yet positive net migration is followed by a downward trend, and negative values are expected to be reached around 2005. A turning point will be reached in 2015, when the increased attractiveness of the region will begin to have an effect on international migration. Around 2030 net migration will be positive again and will continue to increase until 2050. Since natural growth is stronger in absolute terms, the net result in terms of population growth is negative for the entire period. As in the east under the Uniformity scenario, opposite developments are expected for both components of change in central Europe as well. In this region, however, natural growth and net migration will be more or less balanced, resulting in only minor changes in total population.

Under the Diversity scenario, the expected trends in natural growth are more homogeneous than under the Uniformity scenario, although at different levels. Overall, the number of births will drop significantly as a result of decreasing numbers of women in the fertile age category. The downward trend is very strong in all regions, ranging from minus 25 per cent in the Nordic countries to as much as minus 70 per cent in the eastern region. At the same time, in all regions except the east, the number of deaths will gradually increase as the moderate increase in life expectancy cannot compensate for the increasing

number of elderly people. Consequently, natural growth will decline significantly in all regions. In eastern Europe, the decrease in the number of elderly
people, which is set to continue until about 2015, will cause a decline in the
number of deaths by 10 to 15 per cent compared with the present situation.
As the number of births is expected to fall considerably, natural growth in the
east will also drop sharply. By 2050, natural growth is expected to vary from
minus five per thousand of the population in the north to minus 17 (!) in the
east. Net migration is assumed to be moderately positive in the north, west
and south, and slightly negative in central and eastern Europe. The impact of
migration on population change will be minor, however, compared with the
impact of the strong negative natural growth.

7.4 | Ageing

Due to the fertility decline on the one hand and the increase in life expectancy
on the other, the age structure of Europe has changed significantly over the
past 20 years. Today, the base of the age pyramid is smaller than the middle
section. In other words, the younger generation is smaller in number than the
middle-age (baby-boom) generation. In the next decades, this large baby-boom
generation will shift further upwards in the age pyramid and pass retirement
age. This ageing process is inevitable and will occur regardless of the scenario
adopted (*Figure 7.7*). Only the timing and intensity of the process vary
between regions and countries.

A simple measure that reflects the ageing process is the mean age of the
population (*Figure 7.8*). The mean age in the 33 European countries is at
present almost 38. This will increase until 2050 to almost 46 under the
Uniformity scenario and to over 48 under the Diversity scenario. Currently
the central and eastern regions have, on average, the youngest population, with
a mean age of 36, and southern Europe has the oldest, with a mean age of over
39. The central and eastern regions will age fastest, however. In both scenarios
they will surpass the northern and western region in the 2020s, and the eastern
region will eventually surpass the southern region as well, to become the oldest
region with an average age of over 47 under the Uniformity scenario and
almost 50 under the Diversity scenario. Northern Europe will be the youngest
region from the 2020s onwards, with an average age of 43 (Uniformity) and
45 (Diversity) in 2050.

Figure 7.7. Population pyramids (proportion of one-year age groups)
a. Europe - Uniformity

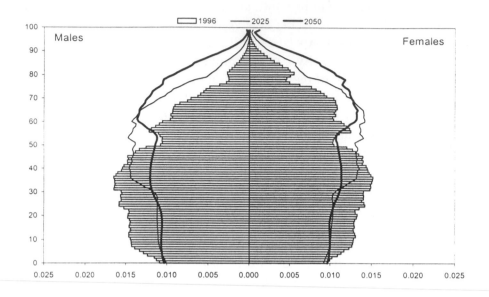

b. Europe - Diversity

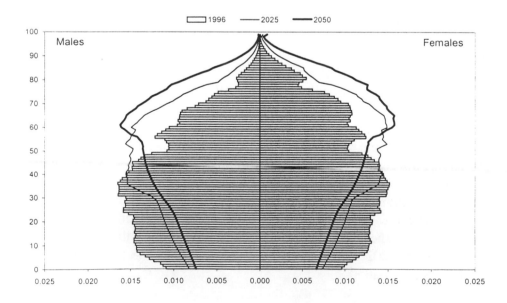

Figure 7.7. Population pyramids (proportion of one-year age groups) (continued)
c. North - Uniformity

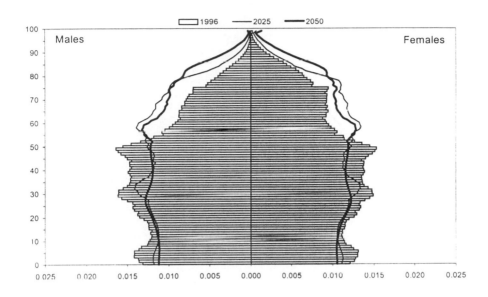

d. North - Diversity

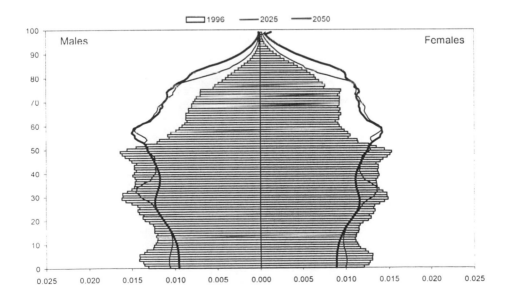

Figure 7.7. Population pyramids (proportion of one-year age groups) (continued)
e. West - Uniformity

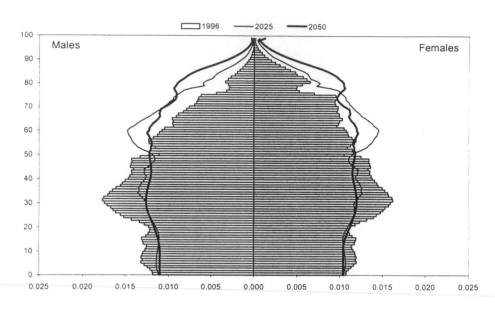

f. West - Diversity

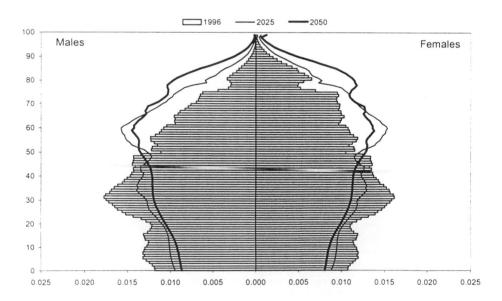

Figure 7.7. Population pyramids (proportion of one-year age groups) (continued)
g. South - Uniformity

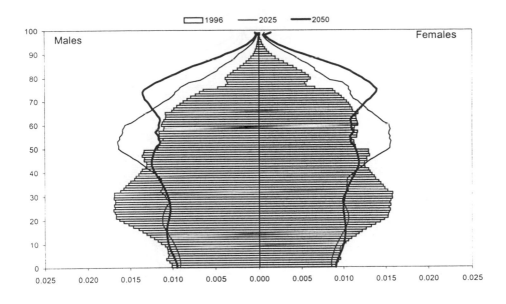

h. South - Diversity

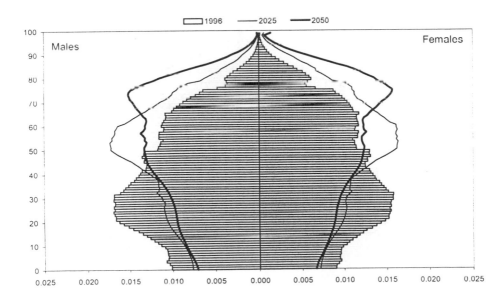

Figure 7.7. Population pyramids (proportion of one-year age groups) (continued)
i. Central - Uniformity

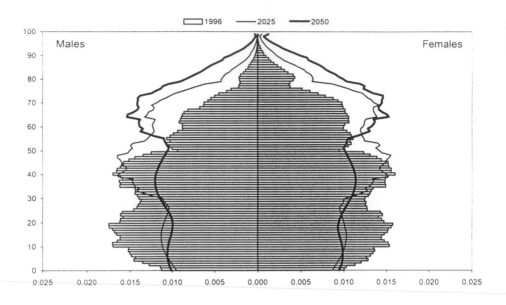

j. Central - Diversity

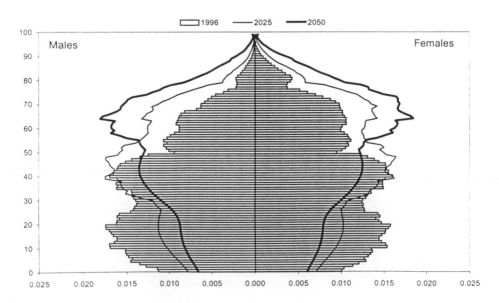

Figure 7.7.   Population pyramids (proportion of one-year age groups) (end)
k. East - Uniformity

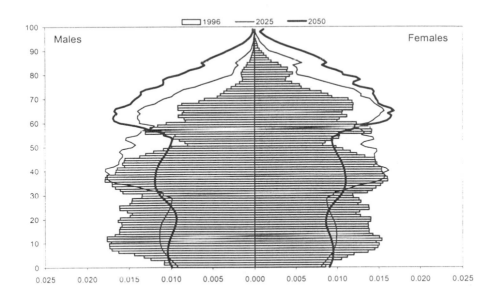

l. East - Diversity

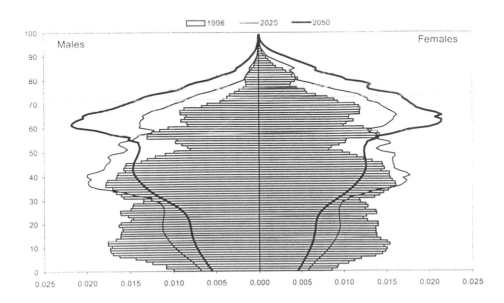

Figure 7.8. Mean age, 1996-2050

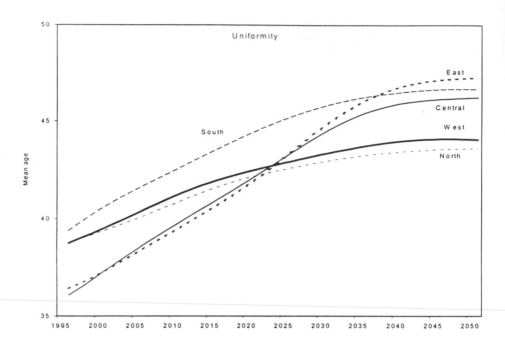

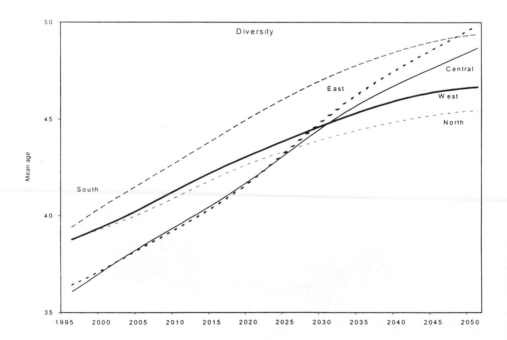

In general, roughly similar ageing trends have taken place throughout the different clusters, but differences remain. In the EEA countries, in both scenarios, for example, by 2025 the largest age category will be around the age of 60. In 2050 under the Uniformity scenario the age structure will be more or less rectangular. Under the Diversity scenario the age structure is more urn-shaped. In the southern cluster under both scenarios a peak is visible above the age of 70. Apart from the effect of the large baby-boom generation on ageing, which is called bottom-up ageing (the inflow of large generations into retirement) there is another cause of ageing which is called top-down ageing: the elderly live longer, which results in an increase in the oldest age categories. This type of ageing is most clearly visible under the Uniformity scenario in eastern and central Europe, where life expectancy is currently relatively low and strong increases are expected for the future, resulting in an increase in the size of the upper section of the age pyramid.

In terms of absolute numbers of elderly, in all clusters the population aged 60 years and over will grow strongly under both scenarios. In eastern Europe under the Uniformity scenario, despite an initial decrease around the turn of the century, this category is even expected to double in size (*Figure 7.9*). This is mainly caused by the strong increase in life expectancy in these regions. In the other regions, the increases will not be much smaller. In northern, western and southern Europe, however, the trend is set to change after 2030, when the less numerous baby-bust generations born in the early 1970s pass the age of 60 and members of the baby-boom generation begin to die. As a result of this change, the growth of the elderly generation in western Europe will be marginal after 2030, in northern Europe it will be zero, and in the south it is even set to become negative. Under the Diversity scenario, the population aged 60 years and over will grow somewhat less strongly than under the Uniformity scenario. This may be attributed primarily to lower life expectancies, in particular in eastern and central Europe. According to this scenario, the elderly population will start to decrease after the year 2030, not only in the south, but also in the west and the north.

7.5 | Dejuvenation

As the number of young people aged 0-19 is largely determined by the birth figures of the past 20 years, we may gain a good understanding of the future development of the size of the young generation by studying the current trend

Figure 7.9. Population 60 years and over, 1996-2050

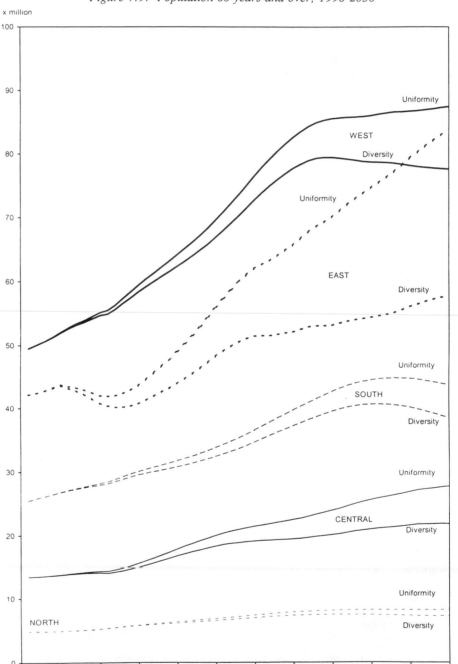

in the number of births. In previous decades, these numbers fell dramatically, and the most important reason for this decline is the decrease in fertility levels. The number of live born children, however, is not only determined by the average number of children a woman will bear, but also by the size of the population of women in the fertile age category (about 15-50 years old). In general the number of births fluctuates with a periodicity of about 30 years, which is the average time required by a generation for reproduction. A large generation will have a relatively large generation of offspring.

Under the Uniformity scenario, initially the development of the number of births appears to be rather similar in the clusters. On closer examination, however, there are notable differences. In northern and western Europe there is a slightly increasing trend between 1996 and 2050 (*Figure 7.10*). Nevertheless, in spite of a small increase in the fertility rate, the number of live born children at first decreases slightly as a result of the declining female population aged 15 to 50. After a few decades, however, the higher birth rate increases the number of births, which is strengthened by the growing size of the number of potential mothers. This is partly due to large net immigration flows. In southern Europe the basic trend is stable, around 1.2 million live births, but there are fluctuations in births which reflect the different sizes of the generations of mothers. Apparently, quite a strong growth in the birth rate compensates for the decline of the fertile population. In central and eastern Europe on average a downward trend is visible, but an increase does take place until 2010, and this is caused by the combination of an increasing birth rate and an increasing fertile population. After 2010 however, the number of potential mothers decreases and consequently for both regions in 2050 the number of births will be about ten per cent lower than in 1996. Under the Diversity scenario, the decrease in the number of births is strong in all regions, but most dramatic in eastern Europe. Whereas under this scenario the total number of live births in Europe will drop by as much as 45 per cent, in the eastern region the current number of births of 2.2 million will drop to 0.7 million! Here, the effects of the low level of fertility and the reduction in size of the fertile age groups point in the same direction, with the result that for every three children born today in the east there will only be one baby born in 2050.

The pattern of young people under the age of 20 is highly similar to that of live born children (*Figure 7.11*), although there are some interesting differences. Under the Uniformity scenario, in eastern Europe the number of

Figure 7.10. Live born children, 1996-2050

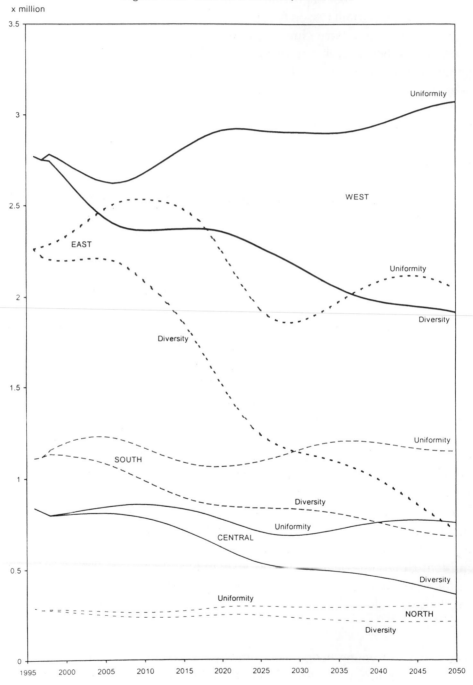

Figure 7.11. Population 0-19 years, 1996-2050

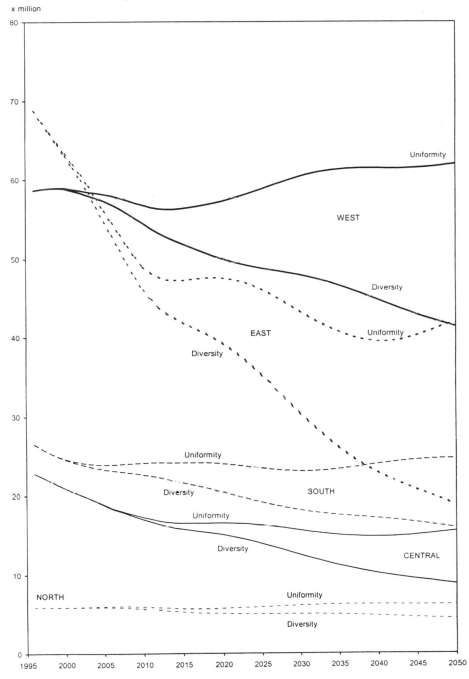

young people drops from almost 70 million at present to below 50 million in 2050, a reduction of 40 per cent, while the number of births fluctuates, but decreases overall by less than 20 per cent. Here, decreases in the numbers of the young are assumed to level off after 2010 as the numbers of births are expected to increase in the near future. In contrast, under the Diversity scenario in the eastern region, an almost linear downward trend in the number of the young is expected, due to lower fertility levels followed by a decline in the female population of fertile age. In absolute numbers a decrease from 70 to 20 million young persons is expected, which compares well with the expected decrease in the number of births in this region. In the other regions the trends are expected to be less dramatic under both scenarios. Under the Uniformity scenario the number almost stabilises in the south and decreases steadily in the central region, whereas under the Diversity scenario both regions experience significant decreases, resulting, in the central region, in the numbers of the young being halved in 2050. In northern and western Europe the size of the young age category is expected to increase slightly under the Uniformity scenario, but under the Diversity scenario, on the other hand, the numbers are assumed to decrease significantly. But this is not surprising, since the expected birth rates under this scenario are well below replacement level.

In summary, differences between both scenarios in the number of births and the young are significant in all regions. On the one hand stabilisation or modest increases will be observed under the Uniformity scenario, on the other hand significant decreases will be observed under the Diversity scenario. The decrease to be observed in eastern Europe is nothing short of dramatic, even under the Uniformity scenario, but it is twice as large under the Diversity scenario.

7.6 | The Working-Age Population

In general in Europe, the number of people of working age (approximated by the population aged 20-59) has been growing for the past 50 years. In the near future this growth will slow down and eventually become negative in almost all clusters, and in both scenarios (*Figure 7.12*). Only in northern Europe under the Uniformity scenario the working-age population remains in growth during the entire period until 2050. The decline will start in southern Europe, followed by central Europe. Negative growth of the working-age population

Figure 7.12. Population 20-59 years, 1996-2050

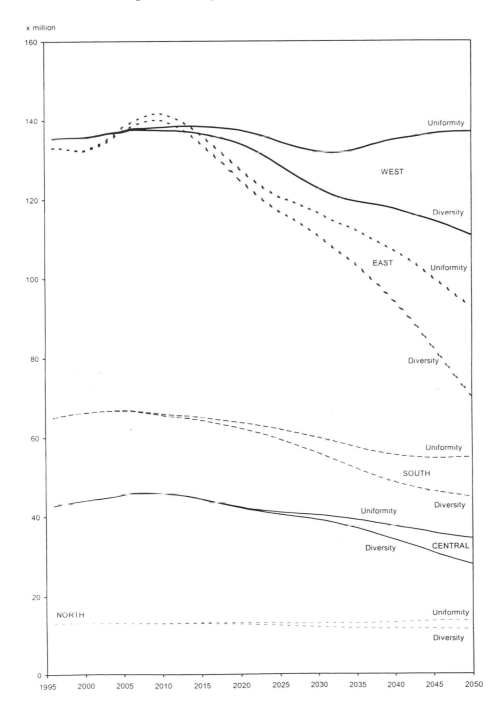

will occur last in the western region, around 2020. Not surprisingly, the differences between the two scenarios will only become apparent after 20 years, when the expected birth generations of different sizes penetrate this age category. For all except the western region the differences between both scenarios are relatively small, especially in the first quarter of the 21st century. In the western region the difference between both scenarios will become significant after 2030, when under the Uniformity scenario the working-age population starts to increase again, while under the Diversity scenario a further decline is expected. Eastern Europe shows a quite different pattern: at first a short decline, followed by a substantial increase until 2015 to 140 million in both scenarios, and finally a strong decrease of about 40 per cent under the Uniformity scenario, and about 50 per cent under the Diversity scenario. This pattern is caused by relatively small birth generations in the past together with net migration outflows. For the size of this age group, international migration is very important. It may for instance compensate to some extent for the declining size of young generations. At the moment this is the case for countries in western Europe such as Germany, France, and the Netherlands.

According to the Diversity scenario, the number of people in all clusters aged 20-59 will decrease in the long run. At first, however, a small increase will take place. In particular in the east a sharp and persistent decline is expected from 2010 onwards, and by 2050 the size of the population of working age will be halved! Given the perspective of the expected developments in the number of young people and births in this region this extreme outcome should no longer surprise us too much. In the other regions the decreases are also manifest, but less dramatic.

7.7 | Age Dependency Ratios

Frequently the relative size of the young and the old in relation to the working-age population is studied because this gives a measure for the 'burden' on the working people of raising the younger generation and caring for the old generation. The ratios, in this case 0-19 / 20-59 and 60+ / 20-59, are usually called the young and old-age dependency ratios, or green and grey pressure respectively. The latter indicators are expressed as the number of children and elderly people per 100 persons of working age respectively. This expression will also be used here.

The pattern of green pressure over time varies according to cluster and there are differences between both scenarios. Not surprisingly higher values (more children per head in the working-age category) will be found under the Uniformity scenario. According to this scenario in western and northern Europe the pressure of the young remains quite constant in the scenario period, around a value of 45 (*Figure 7.13*). In the southern region, the current value is about 40 but this will decrease until about 2005. In the following decades the level will be relatively stable, but after 2030 it increases to the western and northern European level. This pattern is caused by the present low fertility levels which take some time to adjust to the higher average European level. A more or less similar but more pronounced pattern can be seen for eastern and central Europe: initially a decrease until 2010, followed by an increase, albeit with some fluctuations and temporary decreases. In 2050 the figure is about 45 all over Europe. Thus the Uniformity scenario does result in uniform European levels. under the Diversity scenario the green pressure stabilises or decreases, due to the relatively lower fertility rates everywhere. In the northern, western, and southern regions a moderate decrease takes place to values between 35 and 40. In the eastern and central regions the decrease is much more pronounced, which leads to values of 28 and 32 in 2050 respectively.

The grey pressure shows more differences between the clusters. Although currently the figures in the clusters are not very different (between 31 and 40), large differences will develop after 2005. According to the Uniformity scenario, in 2050 the figures will range from 61 (north) to 90 (east), whereas for all the countries under study taken as a whole the figure will be 75. The European value under the Diversity scenario is very similar to this number, i.e. 77 (*Figure 7.14*). As developments are similar in both scenarios, the European population will age at a pace that is independent of the developments in fertility, mortality and migration. When studying the cluster figures, however, it becomes clear that different developments take place in the clusters which compensate for each other in the aggregate. In both scenarios, in the northern and western regions grey pressure increases from 40 to about 60 in 2030. After 2030 the populations age faster under the Diversity scenario. Under the Uniformity scenario the increase of the proportion of elderly people will be moderated by the relatively large inflow of young people. The southern region already has a relatively high share of elderly people and the figure will rise to a maximum of about 80 in 2040.

Figure 7.13. Green pressure

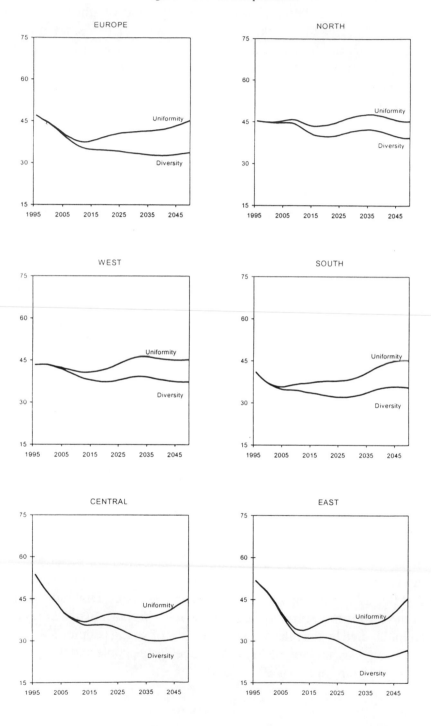

Figure 7.14. Grey Pressure

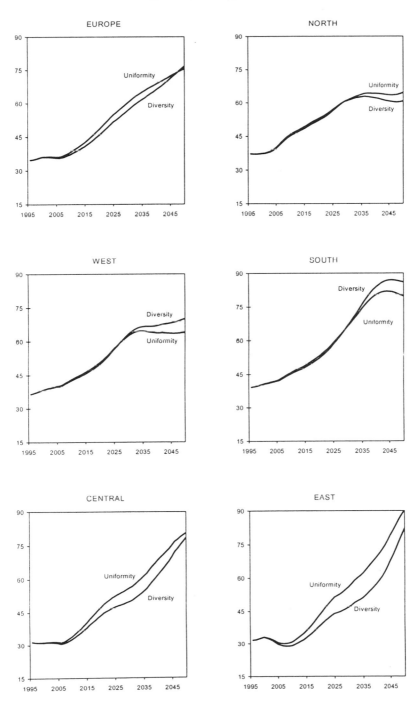

For central and eastern Europe the picture is rather different. These regions start at a somewhat lower level than the EEA countries, but due to low birth rates in the recent past and in the near future, the grey pressure will increase strongly after 2005. In 2050 it exceeds the level in western and northern Europe. The grey pressure in eastern and central Europe increases faster under the Uniformity than under the Diversity scenario, although, when approaching 2050, the difference decreases. Apparently, the impact of increasing life expectancy will be felt at an earlier point in time than the impact of the increase in birth rates.

7.8 | Population Developments in the Individual Clusters

Whereas in the previous sections various aspects of the results of the scenarios were presented jointly for all clusters, in this section we will focus on the results for each cluster individually. This may give a more comprehensive understanding of the demographic developments within each cluster.

7.8.1. Northern Europe or the Maternalistic Cluster

Under the Uniformity scenario all northern countries will experience a continuous increase in population. This is largest for Iceland, which in 2050 will have a population that is 37 per cent larger than in 1996 (see also Figure 7.4). The increase for Sweden is relatively modest: 12 per cent. Under the Diversity scenario the population of Sweden grows only slightly in the first few years, but soon the population starts to decline and already in 2010 the population is slightly smaller than at present (see also Figure 7.5). In 2050 the total loss will be ten per cent. The populations of the other countries under the Diversity scenario increase for many decades. In 2010 they are on average five per cent higher than at present. The population of Finland starts to decline after about 2020 and in 2050 the size is somewhat lower than today. The populations of Iceland, Denmark and Norway start to decline only at the end of the scenario period. By then, their populations will still be larger than in 1996.

Under the Uniformity scenario in general, the effects of large positive net migration and positive natural growth work in the same direction, in particular in the short term. With the exception of Iceland, in all countries eventually natural growth becomes negative. Apart from in Sweden, this occurs far in the next century. Under the Diversity scenario both natural growth and net migration are lower than under the Uniformity scenario. In Sweden, natural growth declines rapidly and relatively soon the positive net migration cannot compensate for this negative natural growth anymore. In the other Nordic countries similar developments start at a later point in time.

As the populations are ageing, all Nordic countries will face an increase in the old population and a decline in numbers of young people. Consequently there is an increase in grey pressure. However, there are quite large differences in the starting situation (*Figure 7.15*) which will persist to some extent in the future. As the differences between the two scenarios are not large, only results for one scenario, the Diversity scenario, are presented. Under this scenario many countries face poor economic development. The presence of many old people can be a heavy burden on society in these circumstances. Currently, grey pressure ranges from about 30 (Iceland) to 40 (Sweden) in the northern countries. In 2050 under the Diversity scenario it will be around 60 (Denmark) to 70 (Sweden). The figure for Iceland will even double.

7.8.2. *Western Europe or the Pragmatic Cluster*

Under the Uniformity scenario all countries except Switzerland will experience a continuous population increase. In particular in Ireland and Luxembourg the growth is large: 47 and 38 per cent respectively. Even under the Diversity scenario the population of these two countries will grow during almost the entire period until 2050. Around 2030 both countries will have a population that is 16 per cent higher than at present. The population of other countries will grow for several decades (France, Netherlands, and United Kingdom), only for a short time (Germany, Belgium, and Switzerland), or hardly at all (Austria). Austria is the only western country that, according to the Diversity scenario, will already lose population in the short term. In 2050, Austria, Belgium, Germany and Switzerland will have a population that is more than ten per cent smaller than today.

The differences in population developments in the western region are mainly due to dissimilarities in natural increase. Germany, for instance, has considerable negative natural growth in both scenarios. Under the Uniformity scenario the positive net migration can easily compensate for this, but under

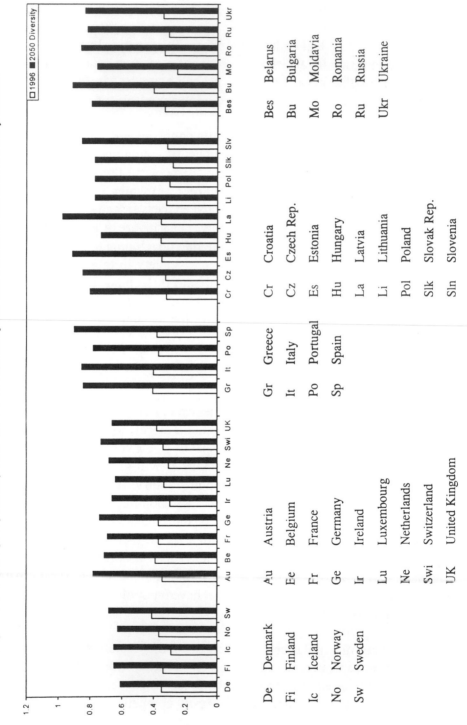

Figure 7.15. Old age dependency ratio (60+ / 20-59), European countries, 1996 and 2050 Diversity scenario

the Diversity scenario this stops after 2010. In the middle of the next century natural increase is strongly negative: the number of deaths in Germany is about half a million greater than the number of births, whereas net migration is only slightly over 100 thousand. Austria and Belgium have higher natural growth, but smaller net migration figures and the result is a population development rather similar to Germany. Switzerland also has low population growth. Neither the birth rate nor net immigration are high. The United Kingdom, France and the Netherlands show somewhat larger population growths. The UK and France have relatively high current birth rates that amplify natural growth. In the Netherlands the population is not as aged as elsewhere and therefore the number of deaths is relatively small.

The relatively large population growth of Ireland in both scenarios is primarily due to the high fertility rate, but growing positive net migration carries ever more weight and is most important for population growth after 2030. The relatively large population growth of Luxembourg is primarily due to high positive net migration. Its natural increase, however, is also relatively high compared to other western countries.

As the birth rate in both scenarios is below the replacement level of 2.1 children per woman, it is not surprising that even in Ireland the age dependency of the young is decreasing, though much less than elsewhere. Grey pressure in western countries currently ranges from about 30 (Ireland) to 40 (Belgium). In 2050 under the Diversity scenario this will be almost 65 (Luxembourg) to 80 (Austria). For most countries the figure doubles.

7.8.3. *Southern Europe or the Paternalistic Cluster*

Compared to the developments in the northern and western regions, in the southern region a relatively small increase in population size is projected under the Uniformity scenario and a relatively large decrease under the Diversity scenario. These results are mainly due to negative natural growth, which is caused by the low birth rate in the Mediterranean countries. In the short term, however (up to 2010), all southern countries will have larger populations than at present, even under the Diversity scenario. The population growth under the Uniformity scenario is greatest in Portugal (by 2050 a total increase of 13 per cent) and smallest in Italy (two per cent), which may reflect the fact that in Italy the birth rate has been low since the seventies. Italy is the most industrialised nation of the Mediterranean countries, which may account for its position. Portugal has a somewhat larger natural increase as the current birth rate is higher than in the other southern countries. As the population ages, the number of deaths increases and it is therefore not surprising that natural growth becomes more negative over time.

Given the negative natural growth, migration becomes very important in retaining the size of the population. Under the Uniformity scenario, it is assumed that net migration is relatively high compared to other European countries due to the particular attractive features of the region, such as the mild climate. Under the Diversity scenario migrants are supposed to be less numerous than under the Uniformity scenario. Despite positive net migration in this scenario, Italy loses almost 20 per cent of its population until 2050, whereas the loss for Portugal is less than ten per cent. Spain and Greece have values in between these two.

Currently, grey pressure is almost 40 for all southern countries. In 2050 under the Diversity scenario this will in general be twice as high: around 80. For Spain the figure will even reach 90.

7.8.4. Central Europe or the Intermediate Cluster

In some ways, the central region is quite heterogeneous. For instance there are diverse prevailing religions and old historical bonds are widely differing. There are Baltic states which traditionally have many contacts with Scandinavia and countries which once belonged to the Austrian-Hungarian empire. All these countries have had a communist regime in the recent past, but some circumstances were different, which still has consequences for their present situation. For instance Hungary had relatively large economic autonomy. Therefore it is no coincidence that the countries that lie closest to the West probably will join the European Union sooner than the more eastern countries.

The intermediate status of this region is reflected in the results of the scenarios. Two of the three Baltic states, Latvia and Estonia, have a demographic development that resembles much that of the eastern region. Even under the Uniformity scenario the population decreases by about 15 per cent in the next 50 years. Under the Diversity scenario the decrease will be 40 per cent or more. Both countries already experience highly negative natural growth, compared to the other countries in this cluster. Moreover they have large negative net international migration. These demographic characteristics reflect a social and economic setback that is similar to that in the eastern region.

According to the Uniformity scenario, however, the population size of the majority of the central European countries decreases at a more moderate pace. Poland and the Slovak Republic will even experience modest growth. Both countries are experiencing positive natural growth today which, even under the Diversity scenario, will remain positive for the next few decades and is mainly due to high birth rates. Moreover, their net migration is only slightly negative. The third Baltic state, Lithuania, shows figures that are more similar to those of neighbouring Poland than to those of the other Baltic countries in the north. A major difference however, is the modest natural decline in both scenarios.

The other countries, Croatia, Slovenia, the Czech Republic and Hungary, are more or less average in this cluster. Croatia currently has positive natural growth, but negative net migration; the Czech Republic shows the opposite. In Hungary in particular natural growth is negative. Under the Uniformity scenario these four countries experience a population decline of around ten per cent, under the Diversity scenario of around 30 per cent.

Currently, grey pressure in the central European countries is around 30 (for the Slovak Republic slightly less). In 2050 under the Diversity scenario it will range from over 70 (Hungary) to almost 100 (Latvia). According to this scenario, in 2050 Latvia will have to face a population of 60 years and over which is as large as the working-age population. This is partly compensated for by the decreasing level of green pressure, from currently over 50 per cent to 30 per cent under the Diversity scenario.

7.8.5. *Eastern Europe or the Post-totalitarian Cluster*

In this cluster, in comparison to the other clusters major population developments will take place, regardless of the scenario. Even under the Uniformity scenario, in contrast with the majority of other countries, the population of all eastern countries but one, Moldavia, is decreasing. In Romania the population size in 2050 is almost the same as in 1996, but Belarus and Russia experience a decrease of about ten per cent and in Bulgaria and the Ukraine the loss is over 20 per cent, compared to the 1996 situation. Under the Diversity scenario the population decrease is even stronger and more similar among the eastern countries than under the Uniformity scenario. The population in 2050 is between 23 and 40 per cent lower than in 1996. The country differences are mainly due to dissimilarities in natural growth. Belarus, Bulgaria, Russia and Ukraine face the largest negative natural growth.

Under the Uniformity scenario Romania and in particular Moldavia retain their current population size quite well. Romania has greater natural growth than the former Soviet Union countries because of a quite young population and –within the eastern cluster– a relatively high mean birth rate. Neighbouring Moldavia has an even younger population and the number of births, except in the first few years, is greater than the number of deaths.

Net migration in this group of countries is quite different at the moment. Large differences in international migration are caused by factors including the uncertain economic situation and the dissolution of the Soviet Union and its aftermath. For example, many ethnic Russians are moving from other parts of the former Soviet Union in Asia to the Russian Republic. This causes a positive net migration for this country. Other countries, like Ukraine, Romania and Moldavia have more emigrants than immigrants. Under the Uniformity scenario net migration is positive sooner or later, but in most countries this cannot compensate for negative natural growth. Under the Diversity scenario, negative net migration adds to negative natural growth in all countries, but is much less important.

Currently, grey pressure in the eastern countries ranges from 25 (Moldavia) to 40 (Bulgaria). According to the Diversity scenario, in 2050 it will range from over 75 to almost 90. This means that in Moldavia the population over 60 will grow by an approximate factor of three compared to the working-age population. For the other countries the ratio will increase more modestly. In general there is a doubling.

7.9 | Variability in Population Growth in the Scenarios

Based on these expected population trends, the name of the Diversity scenario is more than justified. The differences between the eastern region on the one hand and the northern, western and southern regions on the other, are particularly striking. Although under the Uniformity scenario the differences in growth rates across countries diminish considerably over the period of the scenario, significant and consistent differences remain, especially in the short and medium term. As a result, under the Uniformity scenario too, there remain large differences in population growth across Europe. The standard deviation is a measure of the variability in population growth rates at the country level. It is expressed in the same terms as the growth rate. Under both scenarios it drops from five to about three in the first decade, reflecting the dominant within-cluster convergence under both scenarios. After a slight increase in the next decade the variation in growth rates drops further to less than two under the Uniformity scenario but starts increasing in the Diversity scenario to almost six in 2050. In other words, by the end of the scenario period the variability in population growth is about three times as large under the Diversity scenario as under the Uniformity scenario. Under the Uniformity scenario this variability can be almost completely attributed to natural growth (since net migration rates are almost uniform), but under the Diversity scenario about 30 to 40 per cent is due to differences in net migration rates.

8. One Europe: How Many Different Worlds in the 21st Century?

Joop DE BEER and Leo VAN WISSEN

8.1 | Introduction

At present, both similar and different demographic trends may be observed in Europe. On the one hand, many European countries have witnessed similar demographic trends in recent decades: fertility rates have declined, life expectancy has risen, the number of international migrants has increased, and populations have aged. On the other hand, there are significant demographic differences across European countries. The total fertility rate now varies between about one in some central and eastern European countries and approximately two in the Nordic countries. Male life expectancy varies between 60 years in Ukraine and 77 years in Sweden. Most northern, western and southern countries are receiving substantial numbers of immigrants in excess of emigrants, resulting in net migration rates of one to three per 1000, whereas in central and eastern Europe excess emigration rates of minus three per thousand may be observed. Population growth is positive in most western countries and negative in most eastern countries. The number of people aged 60 or over as a percentage of the population aged 20-59 years varies between 30 per cent in Iceland and Ireland and 40 per cent in Sweden.

A key question for the future is whether Europe will be characterised primarily by similarities or by differences. Unfortunately, we cannot

J. de Beer and L. van Wissen (eds.),
European: One Continent, Different Worlds Population Scenarios for the 21st Century, 149–161.
© 1999 *Kluwer Academic Publishers. Printed in the Netherlands.*

answer this question unequivocally. Instead, we have formulated both a
Uniformity and a Diversity scenario in this book to express our uncertainty
about the demographic future of Europe. In these scenarios we have also
expressed that demographic developments are not isolated processes as
such, but are embedded in the socioeconomic and cultural dimensions of
society. Indeed, the uncertain demographic future of Europe is strongly
linked to the fact that the continent is currently in a transitional phase with
respect to political, economic, social and cultural developments. The
integration process within the framework of the European Union may turn
the continent, including the central and eastern countries, into a more
prosperous and less fragmented region. But there are also major forces
within the participating countries that could obstruct further integration or
even reverse the integration process. Moreover, in central and eastern
Europe the outcome of the process of political, economic and social
transition is still highly uncertain and could lead to a new political set-up
and –once again– a divided Europe. Whatever the outcome, European
society will change substantially in the next decades, giving rise to a
number of major demographic changes.

Changes in demographic trends are themselves not only the result of
societal changes, but they, in turn, tend to have long-lasting effects on
society. For example, an increase in the number of births will affect the
age structure in the subsequent 70 years or more. Moreover, ageing affects
both labour supply and labour demand, while population growth has
important repercussions for the environment. It is therefore important to
assess demographic changes in the long term. To the extent that
demographic developments differ among European countries, separate
countries may face different opportunities and problems. One major
question on the threshold of a new century is therefore whether demographic differences among European countries will become smaller in the
21st century or whether they will persist.

The two scenarios are formulated for 33 European countries and cover the
first half of the 21st century. The scenarios are defined in terms of economic and cultural assumptions. Demographic trends in fertility, mortality
and international migration are determined by these two dimensions. One
scenario, the Uniformity scenario, assumes convergence of economic and
cultural trends in all European countries and, because of their causal
dependence on these trends, developments in fertility, mortality, and

international migration will also converge. Another scenario assumes that differences will persist. This Diversity scenario assumes that five clusters of countries can be distinguished on the basis of economic and cultural differences. The culture in northern Europe is characterised as maternalistic (emphasis on emancipation and modern patterns of family formation), the western European culture as pragmatic (emphasis on economic wealth, neither extremely modern nor conservative), the culture in southern Europe as paternalistic (traditional gender roles), in eastern Europe the culture is characterised as post-totalitarian (no firm legal structure) and central Europe takes an intermediate position between western and eastern and between northern and southern cultures. The Diversity scenario assumes that the continued economic and cultural differences will lead to continued differences in fertility, mortality and international migration.

The aim of this book is to examine the extent to which these alternative assumptions about future developments in fertility, mortality and international migration will lead to differences in population growth and age structure. This chapter summarises the main assumptions underlying the scenarios and the main demographic outcomes. Subsequently possible consequences for economic and cultural developments across European countries will be discussed.

8.2 | Scenario Assumptions

The Uniformity scenario assumes strong economic growth in all European countries, substantial technological progress, a tendency towards an extended European Union, and an emphasis on post-materialistic values. Based on these assumptions, this scenario expects that fertility will be relatively high in all European countries (1.8 children per woman in 2050), that life expectancy at birth will be high (83 years for men, 86 years for women in 2050), and that net migration will be strongly positive (three to four per thousand population in 2050). Convergence of living standards in Europe implies that economic growth will be higher in the central and eastern European countries than in northern, western and southern Europe. Correspondingly, fertility, life expectancy and net migration will rise more strongly in the former regions than in the latter.

The relationship between economic growth on the one hand and fertility, life expectancy and migration on the other is non-linear. Economic growth has a positive effect on the level of fertility, but once the desired level of fertility is reached, a continuation of economic growth will not result in a further increase of fertility. The effect of economic growth on life expectancy is non-linear because of the 'law of diminishing returns'. To the extent that mortality rates are already low, it will become increasingly difficult to achieve further reductions. The law of diminishing returns is also applicable to migration in relation to economic growth. The development of net migration is the sum of separate trends in immigration and emigration. In general, immigration is more responsive to economic growth than emigration. For immigration, the existing large gap in economic development between European countries and many Third World countries is an important attractive factor for immigrants, and the effect of a further increase in the size of this gap will be less than an increase at lower levels of economic development. In addition, high levels of economic development may even stimulate emigration of affluent citizens to attractive regions in Europe.

The Diversity scenario assumes a stagnation of economic growth, particularly in eastern and central European countries, and a continuation of cultural differences. This scenario assumes that economic conditions are the main cause of differences between western and eastern Europe and that cultural differences are the main source of differences between northern and southern Europe. As a result of these assumed economic and cultural trends, fertility rates are expected to be lower than under the Uniformity scenario, ranging from 1.1 in eastern Europe to 1.6 in northern Europe. Life expectancy is also lower than under the Uniformity scenario, ranging from 70 years for men in eastern Europe to 80 years for men in northern, western and southern Europe and, in the same clusters of countries, from 78 years to 84 years for women. Finally, net migration is less positive than under the Uniformity scenario due to restrictive immigration policies regarding migrants from outside Europe. Because of the differences in economic growth, migrants move from eastern and central Europe to northern, western and southern Europe. Hence net migration rates are negative in eastern Europe (minus 1.5 per thousand population) and positive in the western part, in particular in southern Europe (three per thousand). Under the Diversity scenario, fertility, mortality, and migration in countries in the same cluster will eventually reach the same values. In other words, current differences among separate countries in the same cluster will disappear in the long run. The underlying assumption is that on the basis of the five economic and cultural patterns that characterise the five geographical regions, systematic differences in demographic behaviour across countries may be identified. It is assumed that other differences among separate countries within the same geographical regions are temporary.

8.3 | Results

Population growth in Europe has slowed down considerably in recent decades. In both scenarios this downward trend is set to continue. Whereas the Uniformity scenario foresees moderate population growth for Europe as a whole, in several countries, especially in the eastern and central regions, population decline is inevitable even under this scenario. Under the Diversity scenario, population decline is the rule rather than the exception in most clusters. Total European population decline in this scenario is about 20 per cent, which is nothing less than dramatic. Similar population developments on such a large geographical scale are unprecedented in modern history.

Under the Uniformity scenario natural growth is set to decrease and will eventually become negative in all five regions. Population growth during the next 50 years will therefore be due entirely to large positive migration balances. In the short term, natural growth will remain positive in the northern, central and western regions, and turn negative in the southern and eastern regions. In most central and eastern European countries, population size will decline, even though the fertility rate will be considerably higher than the current level. A remarkable result of the Uniformity scenario is that, despite the fact that fertility and mortality levels are expected to become the same for all countries in the long run, population growth will still differ strongly among countries. In the northern and western regions, the population will increase by almost 20 per cent in the next 50 years, whereas the population of eastern Europe will decline by ten per cent. Population growth will be highest in a number of small countries (e.g. almost 50 per cent in Ireland). Looking at the larger countries, population growth will be high in France and the UK (over 20 per cent), whereas the population of Bulgaria and Ukraine will decline by more than 20 per cent. These large growth differentials are due to the substantial differences in the current demographic structures of the various countries, which illustrates the point that differences in demographic structure have long-lasting demographic effects. Under the Diversity scenario, there will be a continuous decline in the population size of most countries. A slight increase during the next quarter of a century will take place only in northern and western Europe, caused by a continued high positive migration balance. For most countries, the question is not whether population decline will occur, but when and at which rate. The decline will be particularly large in eastern Europe. In 2050, population numbers will be 40 per cent below the current level. This prospect of a declining population is a major challenge for the future. Important implications of this development are the problem of maintaining sufficient and adequate levels of services and how to deal with a downturn in economic production.

The size of the working-age population will fluctuate over time. After a slight decline in the first few years, there will be an increase until about 2010 under both scenarios, in all regions except eastern Europe. After 2010, the size of the working-age population will decline in all regions under both scenarios, although the decline will be much larger under the Diversity scenario. The decrease will be dramatic in the eastern region, where a 30 per cent reduction is expected under the Uniformity scenario and a 50 per cent decline under the Diversity scenario. In the western region, the Uniformity scenario foresees a turning point around 2030, after which a modest growth will set in. This turning point marks the end of a period of outflow of the large baby-boom generations from the labour market into retirement. In the southern region a similar turning point will occur after 2040. Note that the Uniformity scenario assumes that strong economic growth in combination with limited population growth and a subsequent decrease in the working-age population will lead to an increase in wage rates. This may have two effects: labour force participation rates may rise, and as a result, even though the growth of the working-age population is set to stagnate, the total labour force may grow. In addition, higher wages may lead to an increase in investments in capital goods and in human capital (such as an emphasis on permanent education), which in turn may lead to higher productivity. We will come back to this issue in Section 8.5.

The size of the school-age population will decline in most regions under both scenarios. In eastern Europe, there will be a particularly strong decrease in the 20 years and younger age group. In northern and western Europe, the Uniformity scenario foresees a moderate decline. Therefore, under the Uniformity scenario no major changes in the supply of educational facilities will be necessary in most countries. Again, eastern Europe is the exception, with an expected decrease of 25 per cent until 2015, and to a lesser extent southern Europe, where a small decrease is expected in the next decade.

Under both scenarios, the number of elderly people will increase strongly in all regions, except in eastern Europe where a temporary decrease in the number of people aged 60 years or over is expected during the first decade of the 21st century. Under the Uniformity scenario, the increase in the elderly population will be larger than under the Diversity scenario, mainly due to the high life expectancy. The difference between the Uniformity and the Diversity scenario is largest in the eastern region. As a result of these developments, the old-age dependency ratio will increase very strongly under both scenarios. In most countries, the ratio of people aged 60 or over to people between 20 and 60 years is between 30 and 40. This ratio will increase to about 80 in southern, central and eastern Europe. In northern and western Europe, the increase will be smaller, but in these regions, too, the ratio will double. The issue of providing adequate levels of services for the elderly, as well as the question as to how future pensions can best be financed will therefore remain on the political agendas of all European governments in the next decades, whatever the demographic future will bring.

Three main conclusions on the demographic future of Europe can be drawn on the basis of a comparison of the results of the two scenarios. Firstly, the population will continue to grow during the next 50 years in most northern, western and southern European countries, while the population is set to decline in most central and eastern countries, even under a scenario in which fertility rates are considerably higher than the current low values. The importance of international migration as a source of population growth is set to increase. Natural growth will be negative in the long run under both the Diversity and the Uniformity scenarios.

Secondly, the ageing of the population will be an issue in all European countries under both scenarios. Its significance differs across regions but for each country it is similar under both scenarios. In central and eastern Europe, ageing will not become a serious problem within the next decade. After 2010, however, the old-age dependency ratio will increase much more vigorously than in the other European countries.

The third conclusion is that, even though there may be a convergence of trends in fertility, mortality, and international migration, there will be significant differences in population growth and age structures among European countries. Differences between eastern Europe and other European countries will be particularly large. In fact, convergence of population growth and age structures would require other demographic developments across European countries than those expected under the Uniformity scenario. This is illustrated by the fact that the differences in population growth between eastern and western Europe are smaller when comparing the Uniformity scenario for eastern Europe (assuming high fertility, life expectancy and net migration) and the Diversity scenario for western Europe (with low fertility, life expectancy and net migration) than when comparing the Uniformity scenarios for both regions.

8.4 | How Realistic are the Scenarios?

In the course of the specification of the scenarios, various simplifying assumptions were made. On the one hand, simplifications are inevitable, since it is impossible to take all the complexities of reality into consideration. A model of reality is by definition a simplified picture of the world, and this is potentially the great strength of a model: to reduce reality to the essential elements which are relevant for the problem at hand. On the other hand, what is essential or not is open for debate. Moreover, an essential factor today may lose its significance in the future, and something inessential in the short term may be very important in the long term.

The European scenarios are based on a number of simplifying assumptions, and, against the background of the results, it is worthwhile reviewing some of them in more detail. First, we assume that there are two basic dimensions in society that determine demographic behaviour: the economic and the cultural dimension. All other determining factors are assumed to be random and need not be taken into account for the future. Therefore, these random factors reduce to insignificance in all scenarios in the future. A corollary of this assumption is that socioeconomic and cultural uniformity implies demographic uniformity of fertility, life expectancy and net migration.

A second assumption is that economic and cultural diversity in Europe will be realised between five clusters of countries. These clusters are assumed to be internally homogeneous. In other words, even in the Diversity scenario there are no economic and cultural differences between countries in the same cluster and all existing differences between countries are due to random factors, which, as stated above, will wane. A consequence of the two assumptions above is that demographic diversity within Europe reduces significantly: within clusters no structural and random variation, and between clusters only structural variation is assumed. Even in the Diversity scenario, in the short term the unifying tendencies within the clusters are dominant. In a later stage, the inter-cluster differences dominate and this may lead to increased variability within Europe. In reality, the European picture will most likely be more diverse than expected in either of these scenarios, and therefore many more different worlds are likely to persist in the next century, but these differences may not be structurally linked to economic and cultural differences.

A third assumption in the Uniformity scenario is that economic and cultural differences will disappear, so that in 2050 we will have a homogeneous economic and cultural European Union which ranges from the Atlantic to the Urals, with uniform demographic behaviour. We are well aware that this is an extremely simplified representation of a complex process of European integration and convergence, of which we lack sufficient knowledge as to how it can actually be achieved. Lacking sufficient knowledge about these mechanisms, we run the risk of being wrong about the consequences of some of the assumptions. What seems inessential today may be important in the long term. The results of the Uniformity scenario, although extremely interesting, do indeed give rise to such concerns. They show that even under complete uniformity there remain large demographic differences within Europe. This in turn, may to some extent invalidate the assumption of a completely homogeneous economic and cultural European area. For instance, the differences in old-age dependency ratios between countries will have consequences for the economic system of these countries. These are incongruities in the scenarios in the long term, to which we will come back below when we discuss feedback effects from population to the economic system. They are the logical result of this simplifying assumption, but they are inevitable until we have more insight into the complexities involved. This is a major task to be left for the future.

8.5 | Implications of the Scenarios

The results of the scenarios show that differences in demographic structures have long-term effects on population growth and age structures. Current demographic differences in Europe will be reflected in substantial variations across Europe in population growth and demographic structures in the first half of the next century, even under strong unifying tendencies. It is important that we assess the political, economic, social and cultural consequences of these different population trends and age structures, because they tend to have a long time horizon as well.

Population growth may put pressure on the environment. This may be an important issue in the densely populated regions in western Europe, since under the Uniformity scenario population growth is relatively strong in this region. In contrast, in eastern Europe both scenarios foresee a steep population decline. Under the Diversity scenario, population numbers are set to decrease continuously. This may induce a negative momentum. Economic development may stagnate due to a decline in both demand and supply. A declining population together with low income levels will reduce the demand for consumer goods. An economic downturn acts as a strong push factor, leading to an increase in emigration and a brain drain to the western countries. This, in turn, has a negative impact on economic growth. As modern societies are built on the implicit or explicit goal of growth, dealing with a substantial population decline and its effects on the economy and on other aspects of society will be a major challenge for most European countries. Under the Uniformity scenario, on the other hand, one might hypothesise that, in addition to the expected migration flows, a combination of population pressures in some western European countries and a substantial population decline in the less densely populated regions of eastern Europe might trigger new migration flows. This is a second-order demographic effect of a scenario which has not been taken into account in the scenario and which we will address in more general terms below.

According to both scenarios, the size of the working-age population will hardly increase in the short term and will decline in the long term. Under the Diversity scenario, there may even be a strong decline. One exception is eastern Europe, where there will be an increase in the first decade of the 21st century. Under both scenarios, however, there will be a dramatic decline in this region after 2010. Under the Uniformity scenario, the stagnating growth of the working-age population may lead to shortages in the labour market. This may give rise to an upward pressure on wage rates. Labour force participation rates may increase as a result. Firstly, there may be an upturn in female participation rates. Note that this scenario assumes an increase in the economic emancipation of women and the availability of sufficient childcare facilities. Secondly, participation rates of elderly people may increase. This may be feasible as this scenario assumes that life expectancy will develop relatively favourably. Thirdly, labour force participation of immigrants may increase. Because of the shortage of labour, immigrants do not restrict the job opportunities of the indigenous population. This may have a positive effect on the integration of immigrants, and is in line with the assumption underlying this scenario that cultural differences will decline. This may not only apply to differences among countries but also to differences among ethnic groups within the same country. In addition, it is assumed that the shortages in the labour market will be a pull factor leading to an increase in immigration. Finally, the rising level of wage rates may bring about technological innovations aimed at increasing labour productivity. Under the Diversity scenario, the declining working-age population is partly or completely offset by stagnating economic growth. In the countries of the European Union economic growth will be positive, but slow. The society will be more traditionally organized, with lower female labour force participation, fewer child care facilities and less integrated immigrants. In the central and –even more so– eastern European countries, the economic downturn may be substantial since capital is a scarce production factor in this region, which limits the potential for increasing the level of productivity. Increases in human capital, brought about by a rise in the educational level, will further the productivity growth. The unequal distribution of power within these countries in combination with the gloomy social and economic prospects may lead to the creation of a small, powerful, and rich elite who controls a large group of have-nots. Ironically, the scenario with the most extreme outcomes would be judged by many as being the more probable of the two. The Diversity scenario is basically an inertia scenario that assumes that current differences will persist. This might well be more realistic than the optimistic assumptions of the Uniformity scenario, namely one common European market and prosperous economic growth across Europe.

While the main economic consequences of demographic developments are fairly clear and in accordance with the general conditions assumed by the Uniformity scenario, the possible cultural implications may be more open to debate. For example, one may assume that ageing may lead to a growing level of conservatism, as the elderly may be assumed to hold more conservative views than young people. Alternatively, one may assume that cohort effects are predominant, and that future elderly people will differ from the elderly today. One important difference between current and future elderly people will be the rising level of education. Another interesting point of discussion may be the extent to which an increase in the size of the population of foreign descent will lead to cultural changes. It remains to be seen whether new cultural trends will develop out of a melting pot of indigenous and foreign cultures, or whether there will be a tendency towards increasingly multicultural, heterogeneous societies.

In discussing the possible consequences of demographic developments it should be noted that the scenarios are primarily based on assumptions about first-order effects of economic and cultural trends on demographic variables. Feedback mechanisms are only taken into account explicitly when specifying assumptions about migration. Feedback mechanisms may arise as changes in fertility, mortality, and migration will lead to changes in population size and age structures. This may have an impact on economic and cultural developments, which may in turn affect fertility, mortality and migration, and so on. In general, it may be assumed that second- and higher order effects will be smaller than first-order effects. Moreover, long time lags may mitigate the effects of the feedback mechanism. For example, changes in fertility affect ageing in the long run only. One exception may be international migration. Migration flows may react quickly to economic developments, and may, in turn, have immediate effects on the economy. For that reason, when specifying assumptions about international migration, some feedback mechanisms have been taken into account. One example is the assumption, in the Uniformity scenario, that the ageing population in southern Europe together with an increase in immigration by retired people will boost labour demand, resulting in a growing number of working-age immigrants. An example of a second-order effect which has not been taken into account was given above, where we hypothesised that the results of the Uniformity scenario might give rise to additional (second-order) migration flows towards the depopulating eastern European countries. This would be in accordance with the open borders of the assumed enlarged European Union in the next century.

The Uniformity scenario shows that even though a convergence of economic and cultural trends may lead to a convergence of trends in fertility, mortality and international migration, significant differences in population growth and ageing across European countries will persist. To the extent that this will lead to differences in economic opportunities and problems across countries and to differences in cultural developments, and to the extent that these differences affect changes in fertility, mortality and international migration, i.e. to the extent that second-order effects are important, individual European countries will be less likely to develop along similar lines. Thus one main conclusion of this study is that even under the Uniformity scenario, which is based on rather extreme assumptions regarding convergence across European countries, Europe will be a continent of many different worlds. Under the Diversity scenario, differences between European countries are set to become even larger.

This discussion leads to an obvious conclusion regarding suggestions for future research. It would be very useful to focus more attention on the possible occurrence of feedback mechanisms between demographic and non-demographic variables. This is particularly important in view of the fact that demographic scenarios tend to focus on developments in the very long term. The longer the period for which scenarios are made, the more likely it is that feedback mechanisms may affect the results.

References

Alders, M.P.C. and D. Manting (1998), Household scenarios for the European Union. *Maandstatistiek van de Bevolking* 46(10), pp. 11-27.

Arango, J. and M. Delgade (1995), Spain: Family Policies as Social Policies. *European Journal of Population* 10, pp. 197-220.

Assael, H. (1992), *Consumer behavior & marketing action*, 4th edition. Boston: PWS-Kent Publishing Company.

Beaujot, R. (1991), Immigration policy and sociodemographic change: the Canadian case. In: W. Lutz, *Future demographic trends in Europe and North America: What can we assume today?* London: Academic Press, pp. 359-378.

Beck-Gernsheim, E. (1997), Geburtenrückgang und Kinderwunsch – die Erfahrung in Ostdeutschland. *Zeitschrift für Bevölkerungswissenschaft* 22 (1), pp. 59-71.

Becker, G.S. (1975), *Human capital, a theoretical and empirical analysis, with special reference to education*. New York: National Bureau of Economic Research.

Becker, G.S. (1993), The economy of looking at behaviour. *Journal of Political Economy* (101), pp. 385-409.

Beine, M. and A. Hecq (1998), Codependence and convergence in the EC economies. *International Journal of Policy Modelling* 20 (4), pp. 403-426.

Blossfeld, H.P. (1995), Changes in the process of family formation and women's growing economic independence: a comparison of nine countries. In: H.P. Blossfeld (ed.), *The new role of women, family formation in modern societies*, Oxford: Westview Press, Inc., pp. 3-34.

Blumberg, R.L. (1984), A general theory of gender stratification. In: R. Collins, *Sociological theory*. San Francisco: Jossey-Bass, pp. 23-101.

Bosveld, W. (1996), *The ageing of fertility in Europe: a comparative demographic-analytic study*. Amsterdam: Thesis Publishers.

Bowlus, A.J. (1997), A search interpretation of male-female wage differentials. *Journal of Labour Economics* 15 (4), pp. 625-657.

Caplow, T. (1998), Trends and contexts: the principle of singularity. *IJCS* 39 (1), pp. 4-14.

Castglioni, M. and G.D. Zuanna (1994), Innovation and tradition: Reproductive and marital behaviour in Italy in the 1970s and 1980s. *European Journal of Population* 10, pp. 107-141.

Chesnais, J.C. (1996), Fertility, family and social policy in contemporary Western Europe. *Population and Development Review* 22 (4), pp. 729-739.

Coleman, D. (1996), *Europe's population in the 1990s*. Oxford: Oxford University Press.

Coleman, D.A. (1997), Converging and diverging patterns in Europe's populations. European Population Conference, Cracow, 10-13 June 1997.

Coleman, D.A. and T. Chandola (1998), Britain's place in Europe's population. In: S. McRae, *Changing Brittain: population and household change in the 1990s* (forthcoming).

Council of Europe (1998), Recent demographic developments in Europe, 1998. Strasbourg.

Day, L.H. (1995), Recent fertility trends in industrialized countries: toward a fluctuating or a stable pattern. *European Journal of Population* 11, pp. 275-288.

Day, G.S., A.D. Shocker, and R.K. Srivastava (1979), Customer-oriented approaches to identifying product markets, *Journal of Marketing* 43 (4), pp. 8-19.

De Beer, J. (1991), Geboorteontwikkeling wordt beïnvloed door vertrouwen in de economie. *Maandstatistiek van de Bevolking* 39 (9), pp. 25-30.

De Beer, J. (1996), Immigratie kan vergrijzing niet tegenhouden. (Immigration cannot stop ageing) *Maandstatistiek van de Bevolking* 96 (11), p. 9.

De Jong, A.H. (1997), Achtergronden van vruchtbaarheidsontwikkelingen. *Maandstatistiek van de bevolking* 45 (10), pp. 12-24.

De Jong, A.H. (1998), Fertility scenarios for the European Economic Area. *Maandstatistiek van de Bevolking* 46 (7), pp. 11-26.

De Jong, A.H. and H. Visser (1997), Long-term international migration scenarios for the European Economic Area. Luxembourg: Eurostat Working Papers.

De Man, V. and A.H. de Jong (1997), Vrouwen met een hoog inkomen zijn vaker kinderloos. *Maandstatistiek van de Bevolking* 45 (12), pp. 32-38.

Deutsch, F.M. and S.E. Saxon (1998), Traditional ideologies, nontraditional lives. *Sex roles* 38 (5/6), pp. 331-362.

Dinkel, R.H. (1985), The seeming paradox of increasing mortality in a highly industrialized nation: the example of the Soviet Union. *Population Studies* 39, pp. 87-97.

Dogan, M. (1998), The decline of traditional values in Western Europe: religion, nationalism, authority. *IJCS* 39 (1), pp. 77-89.

Duchene, J. and G. Wunsch (1991), Population Aging and the Limits to Human Life. In: W. Lutz (ed.), *Future demographic trends in Europe and North America: What can we assume today?* London: Academic Press.

Easterlin, R.A. (1969), Towards a socio-economic theory of fertility. In: S.J. Behrman, L. Corsa and R. Freedman (eds.), *Fertility and family planning: A world view*. Ann Arbor: University of Michigan Press.

Easterlin, R.A. (1975), An economic framework for fertility analysis. *Studies in Family Planning* 6, pp. 54-63.

Easterlin, R. (1976), The conflict between aspirations and resources. *Population and Development Review* 2 (3/4), pp. 417-425.

ECE (1997), Trends in Europe and North America 1996/97. The Statistical Yearbook of the Economic Commission for Europe. New York: United Nations.

Ellinsæter, A.L. and M. Rønsen (1996), The dual strategy; Motherhood and the work contract in Scandinavia. *European Journal of Population* 12, pp. 239-260.

European Commission (1996), The demographic situation in the European Union, 1995. Luxembourg: Office for Official Publications of the European Communities.

Fassmann H. and R. Münz (1992), Patterns and trends of international migration in Western Europe. *Population and Development Review*, 18 (3), pp. 457-480.

Genov, N. (1998), Transformation and anomie: problems of quality of life in Bulgaria. *Social Indicators Research* 43, pp. 197-209.

Golini, A. and A. Nobile (1991), L'Italie/Italy. In: J.L. Rallu and A. Blum (eds.), *European Population* 1. Country Analysis. Paris, pp. 355-378.

Guinnane, T.W. , B.S. Okun, and J. Trussell (1994), What do we know about the timing of fertility transition in Europe? *Demography* 31 (1), pp. 1-20.

Guo, G. (1993), Mortality trends and causes of death: a comparison between Eastern and Western Europe, 1960s-1980s. *European Journal of Population* 9, pp. 287-312.

Harding, S., D. Phillips, and M.P. Fogarty (1986), Contrasting values in Western Europe: Unity, diversity and change. The European Value Systems Study Group. London: MacMillan Press Ltd.

Hartley, R.F. (1995), *Marketing mistakes*, 6th edition. New York: John Wiley & Sons.

Hoem, J. M. (1993), Public policy as the fuel of fertility: Effects of a policy reform on the pace of childbearing in Sweden in the 1980s. *Acta Sociologica* 36, pp. 19-31.

Hofstede, G. (1984), Culture's consequences: international differences in work-related values. Beverly Hills: Sage Publications.

Hofstede, G. and M.II. Bond (1988), The Confucius connection: from cultural roots to economic growth. *Organizational Dynamics* 16 (4), pp. 4-21.

Höhn, C. (1991a), Policies relevant to fertility. In: W. Lutz, *Future demographic trends in Europe and North America: what can we assume today?* London: Academic Press, pp. 247-256.

Höhn, C. (1991b), L'Allemagne/Germany. In: J.L. Rallu and A. Blum (eds.), *European Population* 1. Country Analysis. Paris, pp. 83-112.

Illner, M. (1998), The changing quality of life in a post-communist country: the case of the Czech republic. *Social Indicators Research* 43, pp. 141-170.

Inglehart, R. (1990), *Culture shift in advanced industrial societies*. Oxford: Princeton University Press.

Jones, G. (1995), *Leaving home*. Buckingham: Open University Press.

Jozan, P. (1991), Changes in Hungarian mortality and the role of the national health program. In: W. Lutz, *Future demographic trends in Europe and North America: what can we assume today?* London: Academic Press, pp. 247-256.

King, R. (1993), European international migration 1945-90: A statistical and geographical overview. In: R. King (ed.), *Mass migration in Europe, the legacy and the future*. London: Belhaven Press, pp. 7-18.

Kocourková, J. (1997), Recent demographic trends in the Czech Republic. *Bevolking en Gezin* 1, pp. 95-112.

Kohler, H.P. (1997), Learning in social networks and contraceptive choice. *Demography* 34 (3), pp. 369-383.

Kuijsten, A.C. (1996), Changing family patterns in Europe: A case of divergence? *European Journal of Population* 12, pp. 115-145.

Kupiszewski, M. (1996), Extra-Union migration: The East-West perspective. In: P. Rees, J. Stillwell, A. Convey, and M. Kupiszewski (eds.), *Population migration in the European Union*. Chichester: Wiley, pp. 13-38.

Landes, D.S. (1969), *The unbound Prometheus: technological change and industrial development in Western Europe from 1750 to present*. Cambridge UK: Cambridge University Press.

Lesthaeghe, R. and J. Surkyn (1988), Cultural dynamics and economic theories of fertility change. *Population and Development Review* 14 (1), pp. 1-45.

Manton, K.G. (1991), New biotechnologies and the limits to life expectancy. In: W. Lutz (ed.), *Future demographic trends in Europe and North America: What can we assume today?* London: Academic Press.

Martin, T.C. (1992), Delayed childbearing in contemporary Spain: trends and differentials. *European Journal of Population* 8, pp. 217-246.

Matutinovic, I. (1998), Quality of life in transition countries: Central East Europe with special reference to Croatia. *Social Indicators Research* 43, pp. 97-119.

McKeown, T. (1976), *The modern rise of population*. London: Edward Arnold.

Meslé, F. and V. Hertrich (1997), Mortality trends in Europe: the differentials between East and West are growing. Proceedings of the International Population Conference Beijing 1997, vol. 2, pp 479-508.

Mincer, J. and S. Polacheck (1974), Family investments in human capital: earnings of women. In: T.W. Schultz (ed.), *Economics of the family. Marriage, children, and human capital*. Chicago: The University of Chicago Press.

Montanari, A. and A. Cortese (1993), South to North migration in a Mediterranean perpective. In: R. King (ed.), *Mass migration in Europe, the legacy and the future*. London: Belhaven Press, pp. 212-233.

Morris, L. (1997), Globalization, migration and the nation-state: the path to a post-national Europe? *British Journal of Sociology* 48 (2), pp. 193-209.

Mulder, C.H. and D. Manting (1994), Strategies of nest-leavers: 'settling down' versus flexibility. *European Sociological Review* 10 (2), pp. 155-172.

Münz, R. (1996) A continent of migration : European mass migration in the twentieth century. *New Community*, 22 (2), pp. 201-226.

Nebenführ, E. (1995), Austra: Heading towards gender equality, and new forms of solidarity. In: H. Moors and R. Palomba (eds.), *Population, family, and welfare. A comparative survey of European attitudes*. Oxford: Clarendon Press, pp. 59-80.

Ní Bhrolcháin, M. (1993), East-West marriage contrasts, old and new. In: A. Blum and J.L. Rallu (eds.), *European Population II. Demographic dynamics*. Paris, pp. 461-479.

Notzon, F.C., Y.M. Komarov, S.P. Ermakov, C.T. Sempos, J.S. Marks and E.V. Sempos (1998), Causes of declining life expectancy in Russia. *Journal of the American Medical Association* 10, pp. 793-800.

Öberg, S. and H. Boubnova (1993), Ethnicity, nationality and migration potentials in Eastern Europe. In: R. King (ed.), *Mass migration in Europe, the legacy and the future*. London: Belhaven Press, pp. 234-256.

OECD (1996), Education at a glance. Paris: OECD Publications.

OECD (1998), Trends in International Migration. Paris: SOPEMI annual report 1998.

Olshansky, S.J., B.A. Carnes, and C. Cassel (1990), In search of Methuselah: Estimating the upper limits to human longevity. *Science* 250, november 1990.

Palomba, R. (1995), Italy: the Invisible Change. In: H. Moors and R. Palomba (eds.), *Population, family, and welfare. A comparative survey of European attitudes*. Oxford: Clarendon Press, pp. 158-176.

Penninx, R. (1986), International migration in Western Europe since 1973: Developments, mechanisms and controls. *International Migration Review*, 20 (4), pp. 951-957.

Pressat, R. (1991), La France, France. In: J.L. Rallu and A. Blum (eds.), *European Population* 1. Country Analysis. Paris, pp. 19-40.

Quellette, J.A. and W. Wood (1998), Habit and intention in everyday life: The multiple processes by which past behavior predicts future behavior. *Psychological Bulletin* 124 (1), pp. 54-74.

Rodrik, D. (1998), Globalisation, social conflict and economic growth. *The World Economy* 21 (2), pp. 143-159.

Roussel, L. (1989). Types of marriage and frequency of divorce. In : E. Grebenik, C. Höhn and R. Mackensen (eds.), *Later phases of the family cycle and demographic aspects*. Oxford: Clarendon Press, pp. 19-36.

Rubery, J. and M. Smith (1997), The future European labour supply. Manchester: European work and employment research centre, Manchester school of Management, UMIST.

Salt J., A. Singleton, and J. Hogarth (1994), *Europe's international migrants: Data sources, patterns and trends*. London: HMSO.

Salt J. and A. Singleton (1995), Analysis and forecasting of international migration by major groups. Paper presented on the international Eurostat/Statec seminar 'New Long-Term Population Scenarios for the European Economic Area' held in Luxembourg, 8-10 November 1995.

Schoen, R, Y.J. Kim, C.A. Nathanson, J. Fields, and N.M. Astone (1997), Why do Americans want children? *Population and Development Review* 23 (2), pp. 333-358.

Schyns, P. (1998), Cross-national differences in happiness: Economic and cultural factors explored. *Social Indicators Research* 43, pp. 3-26.

Scott, J. (1998), Generational changes in attitudes to abortion: a cross-national comparison. *European Sociological Review* 14 (2), pp. 177-190.

Shim, S. (1998), The changing marketplace in the global economy: Implications for future research. *Family and Consumer Sciences Research Journal* 26 (4), pp. 444-461.

Siriopoulos, C. and D. Asteriou (1998), Testing for convergence across the Greek regions. *Regional Studies* 32 (6), pp. 537-546.

Smock, P.J. and W.D. Manning (1997), Cohabiting partners' economic circumstances and marriage. *Demography* 34 (3), pp. 331-341.

SOPEMI (1997), Trends in international migration. Paris: OECD publications.

Stack, S. (1998), Marriage, family and loneliness: A cross-national study. *Sociological Perspectives* 41 (2), pp. 415-432.

Sundström, M. and F.P. Stafford (1992), Female labour force participation, fertility and public policy in Sweden. *Population* 3, pp. 199-215.

The Economist (1998), The ex-communist east: Flickers of economic light. *The Economist*, September 5th, pp. 25-27.

Valkonen, T. (1994), Socio-economic mortality differences in Europe. In: G.C.N. Beets, J.C. van den Brekel, R.L. Cliquet, G. Dooghe, and J. de Jong Gierveld (eds.), *Population and Family in the Low Countries: Late fertility and other current issues*. Lisse: Swets & Zeitlinger, NIDI CBGS Publications No 30, pp. 127-150.

Van de Kaa, D.J. (1987), Europe's second demographic transition. *Population Bulletin* 42 (1), Washington D.C.: Population Reference Bureau.

Van de Kaa, D.J. (1993), European migration at the end of history. *European Review*, 1 (1), pp. 87-108.

Van de Kaa, D.J. (1994), The second demographic transition revisited: theories and expectations. In: G.C.N. Beets, J.C. van den Brekel, R.L. Cliquet, G. Dooghe, and J. de Jong Gierveld (eds.), *Population and Family in the Low Countries 1993: Late fertility and other current issues*. Lisse: Swets & Zeitlinger, NIDI CBGS Publications No 30, pp. 81-126.

Van de Kaa, D.J. (1996a), Anchored narratives: The story and findings of half a century of research into the determinants of fertility. *Population Studies* 50, pp. 389-432.

Van de Kaa, D.J. (1996b), International mass migration: A threat to Europe's borders and stability. *The Economist* 144 (2), pp. 259-284.

Van der Gaag, N., L. van Wissen, E. van Imhoff, and C. Huisman (1999), National and regional population trends in the European Union 1975-2025. Eurostat Working Paper.

Van der Lippe, L. and E. Fodor (1998), Changes in gender inequality in six Eastern European countries. *Acta Sociologica* 41, pp. 131-149.

Van Giersbergen, N.P.A. and J. de Beer (1997), Number of births and consumer confidence: An econometric analysis. *Maandstatistiek van de Bevolking* 45 (11), pp. 23-27.

Van Hoorn, W.D. (1993), Determinanten van sterfte. *Maandstatistiek van de Bevolking* 41 (1), pp. 29-41.

Van Hoorn, W.D. and J. de Beer (1998), Analysis and projection of national and regional mortality for countries of the European Economic Area. *Maandstatistiek van de Bevolking* 46 (6), pp. 8-16.

Van Hoorn, W. and N. Keilman (1997), Births expectations and their use in fertility forecasting. Luxembourg: Eurostat Working Papers E4/1997-4.

Veenhoven, R. (1996), Happy life-expectancy: a comprehensive measure of quality-of-life in nations. *Social Indicators Research* 39, pp. 1-58.

Willekens F.J. (1992), National population forecasting: state-of-the-art and research needs. In: N. Keilman and H. Cruijsen (eds.), *National Population Forecasting in Industrialized Countries*. Amsterdam: Swets & Zeitlinger, pp. 87-104.

Wils, A.B. (1991), Survey of immigration trends and assumptions about future migration. In: W. Lutz, *Future demographic trends in Europe and North America: What can we assume today?* London: Academic Press, pp. 247-256.

WHO (World Health Organisation) (1998), Internet site.

WHO European Centre for Environment and Health (1995), Concern for Europe's Tomorrow: Health and the Environment in the WHO European Region. Stuttgart: Wissenschaftliche Verlagsgesellschaft.

Zvidrins, P. (1998), Changes in living standards and depopulation in Latvia in the 1990s. *Social Indicators Research* 43, pp. 121-140.

Appendix 1

Table A1. Uniformity scenario: total population at 01/01

	* 1000						index 1996 =100
	1996	2000	2005	2010	2025	2050	2050
Denmark	5,251	5,341	5,464	5,580	5,950	6,429	122
Finland	5,117	5,176	5,250	5,334	5,663	5,987	117
Iceland	268	275	283	292	326	368	137
Norway	4,370	4,467	4,580	4,684	5,092	5,557	127
Sweden	8,837	8,867	8,903	8,956	9,443	9,884	112
Cluster North	**23,843**	**24,127**	**24,479**	**24,847**	**26,474**	**28,225**	**118**
Austria	8,055	8,100	8,131	8,169	8,510	8,758	109
Belgium	10,143	10,211	10,288	10,377	10,866	11,426	113
France	58,256	59,258	60,528	61,813	66,301	71,875	123
Germany	81,817	82,463	83,271	84,052	87,283	89,745	110
Ireland	3,616	3,714	3,853	4,022	4,564	5,303	147
Luxembourg	413	433	454	471	519	569	138
Netherlands	15,494	15,844	16,258	16,618	17,862	18,993	123
Switzerland	7,062	7,153	7,227	7,293	7,644	7,827	111
United Kingdom	58,693	59,493	60,423	61,452	66,156	71,850	122
Cluster West	**243,549**	**246,669**	**250,434**	**254,268**	**269,706**	**286,346**	**118**
Greece	10,465	10,554	10,698	10,843	11,095	11,347	108
Italy	57,333	57,674	58,171	58,539	58,890	58,524	102
Portugal	9,921	10,001	10,138	10,286	10,658	11,245	113
Spain	39,242	39,471	39,921	40,437	41,336	42,087	107
Cluster South	**116,961**	**117,701**	**118,928**	**120,105**	**121,980**	**123,203**	**105**
Croatia	4,752	4,727	4,702	4,678	4,563	4,325	91
Czech Republic	10,321	10,284	10,212	10,132	9,820	9,248	90
Estonia	1,476	1,432	1,400	1,383	1,344	1,283	87
Hungary	10,212	10,078	9,952	9,843	9,558	9,407	92
Latvia	2,502	2,407	2,340	2,301	2,232	2,110	84
Lithuania	3,712	3,692	3,672	3,658	3,627	3,568	96
Poland	38,610	38,683	38,834	39,109	39,921	40,086	104
Slovak Republic	5,368	5,404	5,461	5,519	5,610	5,638	105
Slovenia	1,990	1,996	1,995	1,990	1,940	1,828	92
Cluster Central	**78,944**	**78,701**	**78,567**	**78,612**	**78,614**	**77,493**	**98**
Belarus	10,264	10,112	10,011	9,960	9,717	9,253	90
Bulgaria	8,385	8,211	8,007	7,810	7,253	6,601	79
Moldavia	4,335	4,287	4,270	4,295	4,411	4,482	103
Romania	22,656	22,334	22,153	22,120	22,078	22,242	98
Russia	147,332	145,425	144,410	144,100	141,652	135,293	92
Ukraine	50,902	48,936	47,217	45,985	43,501	40,302	79
Cluster East	**243,875**	**239,305**	**236,068**	**234,270**	**228,612**	**218,173**	**89**
Total	**707,172**	**706,502**	**708,476**	**712,101**	**725,385**	**733,439**	**104**

Table A2. Diversity scenario: total population at 01/01

	* 1000						index 1996 =100
	1996	2000	2005	2010	2025	2050	2050
Denmark	5,251	5,334	5,420	5,480	5,585	5,385	103
Finland	5,117	5,171	5,214	5,242	5,247	4,855	95
Iceland	268	275	280	284	292	282	105
Norway	4,370	4,460	4,541	4,595	4,737	4,578	105
Sweden	8,837	8,859	8,845	8,806	8,745	8,017	91
Cluster North	**23,843**	**24,099**	**24,301**	**24,407**	**24,607**	**23,116**	**97**
Austria	8,055	8,095	8,087	8,039	7,841	6,885	85
Belgium	10,143	10,201	10,223	10,200	9,998	8,996	89
France	58,256	59,197	60,080	60,628	60,845	56,476	97
Germany	81,817	82,386	82,754	82,734	81,543	72,973	89
Ireland	3,616	3,708	3,822	3,939	4,173	4,191	116
Luxembourg	413	432	450	463	480	454	110
Netherlands	15,494	15,828	16,145	16,333	16,561	15,200	98
Switzerland	7,062	7,148	7,189	7,183	7,054	6,169	87
United Kingdom	58,693	59,445	60,119	60,610	61,644	58,271	99
Cluster West	**243,549**	**246,439**	**248,869**	**250,128**	**250,139**	**229,616**	**94**
Greece	10,465	10,542	10,610	10,624	10,306	9,169	88
Italy	57,333	57,607	57,690	57,404	54,800	47,204	82
Portugal	9,921	9,994	10,069	10,097	9,879	9,056	91
Spain	39,242	39,428	39,588	39,574	38,211	33,598	86
Cluster South	**116,961**	**117,570**	**117,958**	**117,699**	**113,196**	**99,026**	**85**
Croatia	4,752	4,707	4,621	4,502	3,995	2,977	63
Czech Republic	10,321	10,281	10,206	10,087	9,393	7,238	70
Estonia	1,476	1,426	1,374	1,329	1,177	879	60
Hungary	10,212	10,073	9,912	9,721	8,922	7,063	69
Latvia	2,502	2,398	2,295	2,211	1,961	1,438	57
Lithuania	3,712	3,687	3,651	3,611	3,406	2,735	74
Poland	38,610	38,662	38,702	38,742	37,461	30,353	79
Slovak Republic	5,368	5,399	5,435	5,456	5,288	4,316	80
Slovenia	1,990	1,994	1,992	1,980	1,846	1,408	71
Cluster Central	**78,943**	**78,626**	**78,190**	**77,640**	**73,450**	**58,407**	**74**
Belarus	10,264	10,095	9,918	9,755	8,968	6,546	64
Bulgaria	8,385	8,187	7,906	7,601	6,537	4,371	52
Moldavia	4,335	4,276	4,217	4,167	3,877	2,904	67
Romania	22,656	22,286	21,825	21,317	19,128	13,645	60
Russia	147,332	144,874	141,928	138,910	125,861	91,405	62
Ukraine	50,902	48,895	46,828	44,967	39,129	27,482	54
Cluster East	**243,875**	**238,613**	**232,623**	**226,717**	**203,500**	**146,354**	**60**
Total	707,171	705,347	701,940	696,590	664,892	556,518	79

Table A3. Uniformity scenario: share of population of 0-19 years in total population

	1996	2000	2005	2010	2025	2050
Denmark	23.5	23.8	24.8	24.9	22.4	22.3
Finland	25.4	24.7	23.8	23.3	22.6	22.3
Iceland	32.2	31.0	29.3	27.9	24.2	22.4
Norway	25.6	25.9	26.0	25.4	22.7	22.1
Sweden	24.6	24.2	23.7	22.5	21.9	21.6
Cluster North	**24.8**	**24.6**	**24.5**	**23.8**	**22.3**	**22.0**
Austria	23.2	22.8	21.7	20.6	20.2	20.7
Belgium	24.0	23.5	22.7	22.0	21.5	21.5
France	26.0	25.5	24.6	23.8	22.7	22.1
Germany	21.5	21.5	20.9	20.1	20.7	21.2
Ireland	33.5	31.0	28.1	26.9	25.5	22.7
Luxembourg	23.9	24.9	25.1	24.7	22.9	22.0
Netherlands	24.3	24.3	24.1	23.3	21.5	21.6
Switzerland	23.3	23.1	22.3	21.2	20.4	21.1
United Kingdom	25.3	25.4	24.8	23.8	22.6	21.8
Cluster West	**24.1**	**23.9**	**23.2**	**22.3**	**21.8**	**21.6**
Greece	23.9	22.0	20.6	20.4	19.9	20.3
Italy	21.0	19.9	19.6	19.6	18.7	20.0
Portugal	25.4	23.5	22.4	22.5	20.8	20.7
Spain	24.3	21.6	20.1	20.1	19.4	20.0
Cluster South	**22.7**	**20.9**	**20.1**	**20.1**	**19.2**	**20.1**
Croatia	25.7	24.6	23.0	21.8	21.0	20.5
Czech Republic	26.6	23.6	21.6	20.0	18.3	18.9
Estonia	27.4	25.5	22.8	20.1	20.2	19.5
Hungary	25.9	23.7	22.7	22.0	20.5	20.4
Latvia	27.0	25.3	22.4	19.1	19.2	18.8
Lithuania	28.6	27.2	24.9	22.1	20.4	19.5
Poland	30.9	28.3	24.9	22.4	21.3	20.2
Slovak Republic	31.1	28.2	25.4	23.3	21.0	20.0
Slovenia	25.7	23.4	21.0	19.5	18.7	19.5
Cluster Central	**28.9**	**26.5**	**23.9**	**21.9**	**20.6**	**20.0**
Belarus	28.9	27.1	24.1	20.9	19.9	18.8
Bulgaria	25.0	22.7	20.3	18.3	17.7	18.4
Moldavia	34.7	32.5	28.9	25.1	23.2	20.2
Romania	28.8	26.2	24.2	22.1	21.6	20.4
Russia	28.3	26.7	23.8	20.8	20.2	19.2
Ukraine	27.3	25.8	23.3	20.7	19.6	18.6
Cluster East	**28.2**	**26.4**	**23.7**	**20.9**	**20.2**	**19.2**
Total	**25.8**	**24.6**	**23.0**	**21.5**	**20.7**	**20.5**

Table A4.   Diversity scenario: share of population of 0-19 years in total population

	1996	2000	2005	2010	2025	2050
Denmark	23.5	23.8	24.4	24.2	20.7	19.7
Finland	25.4	24.7	23.6	22.7	20.7	19.5
Iceland	32.2	30.9	28.8	26.9	21.7	19.1
Norway	25.6	25.9	25.7	24.7	20.9	19.4
Sweden	24.6	24.2	23.6	22.1	20.0	18.8
Cluster North	**24.8**	**24.6**	**24.2**	**23.2**	**20.5**	**19.3**
Austria	23.2	22.8	21.5	20.2	17.9	17.0
Belgium	24.0	23.5	22.6	21.5	19.2	17.8
France	26.0	25.5	24.3	23.1	20.1	18.3
Germany	21.5	21.5	20.7	19.5	18.5	17.7
Ireland	33.5	30.9	27.8	26.3	23.1	19.0
Luxembourg	23.9	24.9	24.9	24.0	20.5	18.3
Netherlands	24.3	24.3	23.8	22.6	19.2	17.9
Switzerland	23.3	23.1	22.2	20.8	18.1	17.4
United Kingdom	25.3	25.4	24.8	23.5	20.5	18.3
Cluster West	**24.1**	**23.9**	**23.0**	**21.8**	**19.5**	**18.0**
Greece	23.9	22.0	20.2	19.5	17.5	16.2
Italy	21.0	19.8	19.2	18.7	16.4	16.0
Portugal	25.4	23.5	22.2	21.9	18.6	16.7
Spain	24.3	21.5	19.7	19.2	16.9	15.9
Cluster South	**22.7**	**20.9**	**19.7**	**19.2**	**16.9**	**16.0**
Croatia	25.7	24.6	22.7	21.0	17.6	14.7
Czech Republic	26.6	23.6	21.6	19.9	17.1	14.3
Estonia	27.4	25.5	22.7	19.6	17.8	14.4
Hungary	25.9	23.7	22.8	22.0	18.8	15.3
Latvia	27.0	25.3	22.2	18.6	17.2	13.9
Lithuania	28.6	27.2	25.0	22.2	19.4	15.1
Poland	30.9	28.3	25.0	22.4	19.6	15.3
Slovak Republic	31.1	28.2	25.4	23.2	19.4	15.2
Slovenia	25.7	23.4	21.1	19.4	17.2	14.7
Cluster Central	**28.9**	**26.6**	**23.9**	**21.8**	**18.9**	**15.1**
Belarus	28.9	27.0	24.0	20.7	17.8	12.9
Bulgaria	25.0	22.6	20.1	17.8	15.2	11.8
Moldavia	34.7	32.5	28.7	24.4	19.5	13.1
Romania	28.8	26.2	23.8	20.7	16.8	12.3
Russia	28.3	26.6	23.5	20.1	17.4	13.0
Ukraine	27.3	25.9	23.4	20.6	17.2	12.5
Cluster East	**28.2**	**26.4**	**23.5**	**20.3**	**17.3**	**12.8**
Total	**25.8**	**24.6**	**23.0**	**21.5**	**20.7**	**20.5**

Table A5.   Uniformity scenario: share of population of 20-59 years in total population

	1996	2000	2005	2010	2025	2050
Denmark	56.7	56.5	54.5	52.3	50.4	49.0
Finland	55.6	55.5	55.4	52.7	48.1	48.4
Iceland	52.7	53.8	54.7	54.5	51.4	49.2
Norway	54.4	54.7	54.2	53.0	50.7	48.8
Sweden	53.4	53.6	52.7	51.7	49.1	48.1
Cluster North	**54.8**	**54.8**	**54.0**	**52.3**	**49.5**	**48.6**
Austria	57.1	56.8	56.0	55.8	50.1	46.7
Belgium	54.6	54.5	54.9	54.1	49.3	47.9
France	53.9	54.0	54.7	53.6	50.1	48.3
Germany	57.4	55.7	54.6	55.0	49.0	46.8
Ireland	51.2	53.7	56.1	55.9	53.2	48.4
Luxembourg	57.0	55.7	55.0	54.3	50.7	49.3
Netherlands	57.9	57.5	56.6	54.8	50.1	48.3
Switzerland	57.1	56.5	55.4	54.1	48.5	47.6
United Kingdom	54.2	54.1	54.4	53.9	50.9	48.6
Cluster West	**55.6**	**55.0**	**54.8**	**54.3**	**49.9**	**47.8**
Greece	54.2	54.9	55.5	54.6	50.9	44.7
Italy	56.5	56.3	55.5	53.9	49.9	44.7
Portugal	54.5	55.7	56.2	55.0	52.3	45.8
Spain	54.8	56.7	57.4	56.3	51.7	43.8
Cluster South	**55.5**	**56.3**	**56.2**	**54.9**	**50.8**	**44.5**
Croatia	55.6	54.7	55.1	55.3	49.5	44.8
Czech Republic	55.4	58.2	58.7	57.3	52.6	42.9
Estonia	53.8	54.9	57.1	58.6	52.5	43.2
Hungary	54.7	56.5	56.5	55.9	52.2	45.3
Latvia	53.9	54.7	56.6	58.8	51.8	42.1
Lithuania	54.1	54.4	55.3	57.2	52.4	44.3
Poland	53.3	55.5	58.5	59.3	52.1	44.5
Slovak Republic	53.7	56.4	58.5	59.0	53.4	44.5
Slovenia	56.4	57.6	58.4	58.3	50.6	42.6
Cluster Central	**54.1**	**56.0**	**57.8**	**58.2**	**52.1**	**44.3**
Belarus	53.4	54.6	57.7	60.3	53.0	42.5
Bulgaria	53.6	55.4	56.9	56.9	51.9	41.5
Moldavia	52.2	53.9	57.3	60.4	53.6	45.0
Romania	53.6	55.5	57.3	58.7	54.0	43.5
Russia	55.0	55.5	59.2	61.3	52.4	42.3
Ukraine	54.4	54.7	57.4	59.6	53.1	42.4
Cluster East	**54.5**	**55.3**	**58.5**	**60.5**	**52.7**	**42.5**
Total	**55.0**	**55.4**	**56.6**	**56.8**	**51.2**	**45.3**

Table A6. Diversity scenario: share of population of 20-59 years in total population

	1996	2000	2005	2010	2025	2050
Denmark	56.7	56.6	54.9	53.0	51.9	49.9
Finland	55.6	55.5	55.6	53.3	49.2	48.7
Iceland	52.7	53.9	55.2	55.4	52.7	49.0
Norway	54.4	54.7	54.5	53.7	52.2	49.5
Sweden	53.4	53.6	52.9	52.2	50.4	48.4
Cluster North	**54.8**	**54.9**	**54.3**	**52.9**	**50.9**	**49.1**
Austria	57.1	56.8	56.2	56.3	51.5	46.7
Belgium	54.6	54.5	55.1	54.6	50.7	48.0
France	53.9	54.0	55.0	54.3	51.5	48.5
Germany	57.4	55.7	54.9	55.6	50.7	47.3
Ireland	51.2	53.7	56.3	56.6	55.1	48.7
Luxembourg	57.0	55.8	55.3	54.9	52.2	49.9
Netherlands	57.9	57.5	56.9	55.4	51.7	48.8
Switzerland	57.1	56.5	55.6	54.5	49.7	47.7
United Kingdom	54.2	54.2	54.5	54.3	52.4	49.3
Cluster West	**55.6**	**55.0**	**55.0**	**54.9**	**51.5**	**48.2**
Greece	54.2	54.9	55.9	55.4	52.8	45.4
Italy	56.5	56.3	55.9	54.7	51.6	45.4
Portugal	54.5	55.7	56.4	55.7	54.0	46.8
Spain	54.8	56.8	57.8	57.1	53.4	44.2
Cluster South	**55.5**	**56.3**	**56.6**	**55.7**	**52.5**	**45.1**
Croatia	55.7	54.8	55.5	56.3	52.6	47.4
Czech Republic	55.4	58.2	58.9	58.0	55.7	46.4
Estonia	53.8	54.9	57.4	59.4	54.8	44.8
Hungary	54.7	56.5	56.7	56.5	55.3	48.9
Latvia	53.9	54.7	56.9	59.6	54.0	43.6
Lithuania	54.1	54.4	55.5	57.8	55.3	48.1
Poland	53.3	55.5	58.7	59.8	55.0	47.8
Slovak Republic	53.7	56.4	58.7	59.6	56.2	48.1
Slovenia	56.4	57.6	58.7	59.1	53.8	46.2
Cluster Central	**54.1**	**56.0**	**58.1**	**58.8**	**55.0**	**47.6**
Belarus	53.4	54.6	58.2	61.5	57.4	48.6
Bulgaria	53.6	55.5	57.6	58.4	56.9	46.3
Moldavia	52.2	54.0	57.8	61.7	58.1	49.5
Romania	53.6	55.6	58.0	60.5	59.9	47.2
Russia	55.0	55.6	59.7	62.6	57.1	47.9
Ukraine	54.4	54.7	57.7	60.5	57.3	47.8
Cluster East	**54.5**	**55.4**	**59.0**	**61.8**	**57.4**	**47.9**
Total	**55.0**	**55.4**	**56.7**	**57.1**	**51.5**	**43.1**

Table A7. Uniformity scenario: share of population of 60 years and over in total population

	1996	2000	2005	2010	2025	2050
Denmark	19.7	19.6	20.7	22.9	27.2	28.7
Finland	19.0	19.8	20.8	24.0	29.3	29.3
Iceland	15.1	15.2	16.0	17.7	24.4	28.4
Norway	19.9	19.4	19.8	21.7	26.7	29.1
Sweden	22.0	22.2	23.5	25.8	29.0	30.3
Cluster North	**20.4**	**20.5**	**21.5**	**23.9**	**28.2**	**29.4**
Austria	19.7	20.4	22.3	23.6	29.7	32.5
Belgium	21.4	22.0	22.4	23.9	29.2	30.6
France	20.1	20.5	20.7	22.6	27.3	29.6
Germany	21.0	22.8	24.5	25.0	30.3	31.9
Ireland	15.2	15.4	15.9	17.2	21.3	28.9
Luxembourg	19.1	19.4	19.9	21.0	26.5	28.7
Netherlands	17.8	18.2	19.4	21.9	28.4	30.1
Switzerland	19.6	20.4	22.3	24.6	31.2	31.3
United Kingdom	20.5	20.4	20.8	22.4	26.6	29.7
Cluster West	**20.3**	**21.1**	**22.0**	**23.3**	**28.3**	**30.5**
Greece	21.9	23.1	23.9	25.1	29.2	34.9
Italy	22.6	23.8	24.9	26.5	31.4	35.3
Portugal	20.1	20.8	21.4	22.5	26.9	33.6
Spain	20.9	21.7	22.5	23.6	28.9	36.3
Cluster South	**21.7**	**22.8**	**23.7**	**25.1**	**29.9**	**35.4**
Croatia	18.7	20.6	21.8	22.9	29.5	34.7
Czech Republic	18.0	18.2	19.7	22.7	29.1	38.2
Estonia	18.8	19.6	20.1	21.3	27.3	37.3
Hungary	19.4	19.8	20.8	22.1	27.3	34.3
Latvia	19.1	20.0	21.0	22.0	29.0	39.0
Lithuania	17.3	18.4	19.9	20.7	27.1	36.2
Poland	15.9	16.2	16.6	18.3	26.6	35.3
Slovak Republic	15.2	15.4	16.1	17.7	25.6	35.5
Slovenia	17.8	19.0	20.5	22.2	30.7	37.9
Cluster Central	**17.0**	**17.5**	**18.3**	**19.9**	**27.3**	**35.7**
Belarus	17.7	18.4	18.2	18.7	27.1	38.7
Bulgaria	21.4	22.0	22.8	24.8	30.3	40.1
Moldavia	13.0	13.6	13.8	14.4	23.3	34.7
Romania	17.6	18.3	18.4	19.2	24.5	36.0
Russia	16.7	17.8	17.0	17.9	27.4	38.5
Ukraine	18.4	19.5	19.3	19.7	27.4	39.0
Cluster East	**17.3**	**18.3**	**17.8**	**18.6**	**27.1**	**38.3**
Total	**19.1**	**20.0**	**20.5**	**21.7**	**28.1**	**34.2**

Table A8. Diversity scenario: share of population of 60 years and over
in total population

	1996	2000	2005	2010	2025	2050
Denmark	19.7	19.6	20.7	22.8	27.4	30.4
Finland	19.0	19.8	20.8	24.1	30.1	31.7
Iceland	15.1	15.2	16.0	17.8	25.6	31.9
Norway	19.9	19.4	19.7	21.6	26.9	31.0
Sweden	22.0	22.2	23.5	25.7	29.6	32.8
Cluster North	**20.4**	**20.5**	**21.5**	**23.9**	**28.6**	**31.6**
Austria	19.7	20.4	22.3	23.6	30.6	36.3
Belgium	21.4	22.0	22.3	23.9	30.1	34.2
France	20.1	20.5	20.7	22.7	28.3	33.3
Germany	21.0	22.8	24.5	24.9	30.8	35.0
Ireland	15.2	15.3	15.8	17.1	21.8	32.2
Luxembourg	19.1	19.4	19.9	21.0	27.3	31.8
Netherlands	17.8	18.2	19.3	21.9	29.2	33.3
Switzerland	19.6	20.4	22.2	24.6	32.2	34.9
United Kingdom	20.5	20.4	20.7	22.2	27.1	32.5
Cluster West	**20.3**	**21.1**	**22.0**	**23.3**	**29.0**	**33.8**
Greece	21.9	23.1	23.9	25.1	29.7	38.3
Italy	22.6	23.8	24.9	26.5	32.0	38.6
Portugal	20.1	20.8	21.3	22.5	27.4	36.6
Spain	20.9	21.7	22.5	23.7	29.6	39.9
Cluster South	**21.7**	**22.8**	**23.7**	**25.1**	**30.6**	**38.8**
Croatia	18.7	20.6	21.7	22.7	29.8	37.9
Czech Republic	18.0	18.1	19.5	22.0	27.3	39.2
Estonia	18.8	19.6	20.0	21.0	27.4	40.8
Hungary	19.4	19.7	20.5	21.5	25.9	35.8
Latvia	19.1	20.0	21.0	21.8	28.8	42.5
Lithuania	17.3	18.4	19.5	20.0	25.4	36.7
Poland	15.9	16.2	16.3	17.7	25.4	36.9
Slovak Republic	15.2	15.3	15.9	17.2	24.4	36.7
Slovenia	17.8	19.0	20.2	21.5	29.0	39.1
Cluster Central	**17.0**	**17.5**	**18.0**	**19.4**	**26.1**	**37.4**
Belarus	17.7	18.3	17.8	17.8	24.8	38.5
Bulgaria	21.4	21.8	22.3	23.8	27.9	41.9
Moldavia	13.0	13.5	13.6	13.9	22.4	37.4
Romania	17.6	18.3	18.2	18.8	23.3	40.5
Russia	16.7	17.8	16.8	17.3	25.4	39.0
Ukraine	18.4	19.5	18.9	19.0	25.6	39.7
Cluster East	**17.3**	**18.3**	**17.5**	**18.0**	**25.3**	**39.3**
Total	**19.1**	**20.0**	**20.3**	**21.5**	**27.8**	**36.4**

Table A9. Uniformity scenario: natural growth per thousand of the population

	1996	2000	2005	2010	2025	2050
Denmark	1.4	1.5	1.3	0.7	1.5	-0.7
Finland	2.1	1.6	1.4	1.3	0.4	-0.7
Iceland	8.9	7.9	6.7	5.7	4.2	0.1
Norway	3.7	3.2	2.3	1.8	2.7	-0.7
Sweden	0.1	-0.4	-0.6	-0.5	0.4	-0.9
Cluster North	**1.6**	**1.2**	**0.9**	**0.7**	**1.2**	**-0.8**
Austria	0.9	-0.2	-0.8	-0.9	-0.1	-2.9
Belgium	0.8	0.4	-0.0	-0.1	0.2	-1.7
France	3.3	3.2	2.6	2.1	1.3	-0.8
Germany	-1.3	-0.9	-1.3	-1.1	-1.3	-2.6
Ireland	5.3	5.9	6.5	7.0	3.7	1.3
Luxembourg	3.9	3.2	2.4	2.1	2.5	-0.5
Netherlands	3.3	3.5	2.3	1.6	1.4	-1.6
Switzerland	2.7	1.3	0.2	-0.1	-0.1	-2.6
United Kingdom	1.6	1.1	0.8	1.1	1.8	-0.5
Cluster West	**1.2**	**1.1**	**0.6**	**0.6**	**0.5**	**-1.5**
Greece	-0.2	0.5	0.5	-0.3	-2.4	-4.1
Italy	-0.6	-0.3	-0.8	-1.9	-3.1	-5.3
Portugal	0.3	1.4	1.4	0.5	-0.8	-3.1
Spain	0.3	0.8	1.0	0.1	-2.3	-5.1
Cluster South	**-0.2**	**0.3**	**0.1**	**-0.9**	**-2.5**	**-4.9**
Croatia	0.8	0.8	0.3	-0.2	-2.3	-3.8
Czech Republic	-2.2	-1.4	-1.2	-1.3	-3.3	-4.6
Estonia	-6.0	-4.2	-2.6	-1.6	-3.4	-3.2
Hungary	-3.6	-2.5	-1.8	-1.7	-2.3	-2.6
Latvia	-8.1	-5.5	-3.3	-2.0	-3.4	-4.6
Lithuania	-1.3	-1.1	-0.5	-0.1	-1.5	-3.6
Poland	0.9	0.7	1.7	2.1	-0.4	-2.5
Slovak Republic	1.6	2.1	2.5	2.4	-0.2	-2.7
Slovenia	-0.1	-0.0	0.1	-0.3	-3.3	-5.5
Cluster Central	**-0.6**	**-0.3**	**0.5**	**0.7**	**-1.4**	**-3.0**
Belarus	-4.9	-3.5	-1.6	-0.6	-2.2	-4.2
Bulgaria	-4.6	-5.0	-4.3	-4.0	-5.1	-5.4
Moldavia	-0.2	1.1	3.0	3.8	1.0	-1.4
Romania	-3.3	-1.3	0.3	1.0	-0.8	-2.3
Russia	-5.8	-3.8	-1.6	-0.4	-2.0	-4.1
Ukraine	-8.5	-6.2	-3.9	-2.8	-3.1	-4.5
Cluster East	**-6.0**	**-4.0**	**-1.9**	**-0.8**	**-2.2**	**-4.0**
Total	**-1.7**	**-0.9**	**-0.3**	**-0.1**	**-1.0**	**-2.9**

Table A10. Diversity scenario: natural growth per thousand of the population

	1996	2000	2005	2010	2025	2050
Denmark	1.4	0.6	-0.2	-1.1	-1.1	-4.5
Finland	2.1	1.0	0.2	-0.3	-2.3	-5.0
Iceland	8.9	6.8	4.9	3.8	1.3	-4.7
Norway	3.7	2.3	0.8	0.0	0.0	-4.6
Sweden	0.1	-1.0	-1.8	-2.0	-2.4	-5.3
Cluster North	**1.6**	**0.5**	**-0.5**	**-1.0**	**-1.6**	**-4.9**
Austria	0.9	-0.6	-1.9	-2.6	-3.6	-8.9
Belgium	0.8	-0.1	-1.2	-1.9	-3.2	-7.4
France	3.3	2.4	1.2	0.2	-2.0	-6.4
Germany	-1.3	-1.6	-2.7	-3.1	-4.4	-8.0
Ireland	5.3	5.1	5.0	4.7	0.4	-3.7
Luxembourg	3.9	2.4	1.1	0.3	-0.8	-5.9
Netherlands	3.3	2.8	0.9	-0.2	-1.9	-7.1
Switzerland	2.7	0.9	-0.8	-1.7	-3.6	-8.5
United Kingdom	1.6	0.6	-0.2	-0.5	-1.4	-5.7
Cluster West	**1.2**	**0.5**	**-0.6**	**-1.2**	**-2.8**	**-6.9**
Greece	-0.2	-0.4	-1.3	-2.5	-5.4	-9.8
Italy	-0.6	-1.3	-2.5	-3.9	-6.2	-11.3
Portugal	0.3	0.8	-0.1	-1.5	-3.9	-8.6
Spain	0.3	0.0	-0.7	-2.1	-5.1	-11.1
Cluster South	**-0.2**	**-0.6**	**-1.6**	**-3.0**	**-5.5**	**-10.8**
Croatia	0.8	-0.2	-1.9	-3.5	-8.1	-14.0
Czech Republic	-2.2	-2.1	-2.8	-3.8	-7.3	-13.2
Estonia	-6.0	-4.9	-4.1	-4.0	-8.7	-13.8
Hungary	-3.7	-3.1	-3.5	-4.4	-6.9	-11.4
Latvia	-8.1	-6.4	-5.0	-4.5	-8.8	-15.4
Lithuania	-1.3	-1.9	-2.1	-2.3	-5.9	-12.0
Poland	0.9	0.1	0.4	-0.0	-4.9	-11.4
Slovak Republic	1.5	1.4	1.2	0.2	-4.5	-11.4
Slovenia	-0.2	0.8	-1.6	-2.9	-7.4	-14.2
Cluster Central	**-0.6**	**-0.9**	**-1.0**	**-1.6**	**-5.9**	**-12.0**
Belarus	-4.9	-4.8	-4.1	-4.3	-8.4	-16.5
Bulgaria	-4.9	-6.7	-7.4	-8.3	-11.9	-19.6
Moldavia	-0.2	-0.2	0.5	-0.0	-6.2	-15.2
Romania	-3.3	-3.1	-3.4	-4.4	-8.4	-18.0
Russia	-5.8	-5.3	-4.7	-4.9	-9.1	-16.6
Ukraine	-8.5	-7.2	-6.2	-6.4	-9.5	-17.8
Cluster East	**-6.0**	**-5.4**	**-4.8**	**-5.1**	**-9.1**	**-17.0**
Total	**-1.7**	**-1.9**	**-2.2**	**-2.8**	**-5.5**	**-10.7**

Table A11.   Uniformity scenario: net migration per thousand of the population

	1996	2000	2005	2010	2025	2050
Denmark	3.0	3.0	3.1	3.2	3.5	2.5
Finland	1.0	1.1	1.6	2.2	3.5	2.5
Iceland	-2.0	-1.7	-0.7	0.6	3.5	2.5
Norway	2.0	2.1	2.3	2.7	3.5	2.5
Sweden	1.0	1.1	1.6	2.2	3.5	2.5
Cluster North	**1.6**	**1.7**	**2.0**	**2.5**	**3.5**	**2.5**
Austria	1.0	1.1	1.6	2.2	3.5	2.5
Belgium	1.0	1.1	1.6	2.2	3.5	2.5
France	1.0	1.1	1.6	2.2	3.5	2.5
Germany	3.0	3.0	3.1	3.2	3.5	2.5
Ireland	1.0	1.1	1.6	2.2	3.5	2.5
Luxembourg	9.0	7.3	5.7	4.8	3.5	2.5
Netherlands	2.0	2.1	2.3	2.7	3.5	2.5
Switzerland	1.0	1.1	1.6	2.2	3.5	2.5
United Kingdom	2.0	2.1	2.3	2.7	3.5	2.5
Cluster West	**2.0**	**2.1**	**2.3**	**2.7**	**3.5**	**2.5**
Greece	2.0	2.1	2.3	2.7	3.5	3.5
Italy	2.0	2.1	2.3	2.7	3.5	3.5
Portugal	1.0	1.1	1.6	2.2	3.5	3.5
Spain	1.0	1.1	1.6	2.2	3.5	3.5
Cluster South	**1.6**	**1.7**	**2.0**	**2.5**	**3.5**	**3.5**
Croatia	-2.6	-2.0	-1.3	-0.9	-0.4	2.5
Czech Republic	1.0	0.4	-0.5	-0.4	0.8	2.5
Estonia	-3.0	-1.4	-0.5	-0.3	0.5	2.5
Hungary	0.0	-0.2	-0.5	-0.4	0.8	2.5
Latvia	-3.0	-1.5	-0.7	-0.5	0.5	2.5
Lithuania	0.0	-0.1	-0.4	-0.5	0.5	2.5
Poland	0.0	-0.2	-0.5	-0.4	0.8	2.5
Slovak Republic	0.0	-0.1	-0.4	-0.5	0.5	2.5
Slovenia	1.0	0.4	-0.5	-0.4	0.8	2.5
Cluster Central	**-0.2**	**-0.3**	**-0.5**	**-0.4**	**0.6**	**2.5**
Belarus	1.0	0.9	0.4	-0.3	-0.7	2.5
Bulgaria	0.0	-0.2	-0.7	-1.0	0.1	2.5
Moldavia	-3.0	-2.9	-2.5	-2.0	-0.5	2.5
Romania	-1.0	-1.0	-1.0	-1.0	0.1	2.5
Russia	2.0	1.7	0.9	0.1	-0.7	2.5
Ukraine	-2.0	-2.0	-1.9	-1.8	-0.5	2.5
Cluster East	**0.7**	**0.5**	**0.0**	**-0.5**	**-0.6**	**2.5**
Total	**1.2**	**1.2**	**1.2**	**1.3**	**1.9**	**2.7**

Table A12. Diversity scenario: net migration per thousand of the population

	1996	2000	2005	2010	2025	2050
Denmark	3.0	3.0	2.9	2.8	2.2	1.5
Finland	1.0	1.0	1.0	1.1	1.3	1.5
Iceland	-2.0	-1.9	-1.7	-1.4	-0.1	1.5
Norway	2.0	2.0	2.0	1.9	1.7	1.5
Sweden	1.0	1.0	1.0	1.1	1.3	1.5
Cluster North	**1.6**	**1.6**	**1.6**	**1.6**	**1.5**	**1.5**
Austria	1.0	1.0	1.0	1.1	1.3	1.5
Belgium	1.0	1.0	1.0	1.1	1.3	1.5
France	1.0	1.0	1.0	1.1	1.3	1.5
Germany	3.0	3.0	2.9	2.8	2.2	1.5
Ireland	1.0	1.0	1.0	1.1	1.3	1.5
Luxembourg	9.0	7.2	5.3	3.9	1.7	1.5
Netherlands	2.0	2.0	2.0	1.9	1.7	1.5
Switzerland	1.0	1.0	1.0	1.1	1.3	1.5
United Kingdom	2.0	2.0	2.0	1.9	1.7	1.5
Cluster West	**2.0**	**2.0**	**1.9**	**1.9**	**1.7**	**1.5**
Greece	2.0	2.0	2.0	2.1	2.3	2.5
Italy	2.0	2.0	2.0	2.1	2.3	2.5
Portugal	1.0	1.0	1.1	1.3	1.8	2.5
Spain	1.0	1.0	1.1	1.3	1.8	2.5
Cluster South	**1.6**	**1.6**	**1.6**	**1.7**	**2.1**	**2.5**
Croatia	-3.0	-2.9	-2.8	-2.5	-1.6	-0.5
Czech Republic	1.0	1.0	0.9	0.8	0.2	-0.5
Estonia	-3.0	-3.0	-2.8	-2.6	-1.6	-0.5
Hungary	0.0	-0.0	-0.0	-0.1	-0.3	-0.5
Latvia	-3.0	-3.0	-2.8	-2.6	-1.6	-0.5
Lithuania	0.0	-0.0	-0.0	-0.1	-0.3	-0.5
Poland	0.0	-0.0	-0.0	-0.1	-0.3	-0.5
Slovak Republic	0.0	-0.0	-0.0	-0.1	-0.3	-0.5
Slovenia	1.0	1.0	0.9	0.8	0.2	-0.5
Cluster Central	**-0.2**	**-0.2**	**-0.2**	**-0.2**	**-0.3**	**-0.5**
Belarus	1.0	1.0	0.9	0.7	-0.1	-1.0
Bulgaria	0.0	-0.0	-0.1	-0.2	-0.6	-1.0
Moldavia	-3.0	-3.0	-2.8	-2.6	-1.9	-1.0
Romania	-1.0	-1.0	-1.0	-1.0	-1.0	-1.0
Russia	1.8	1.2	0.6	0.2	-0.2	-1.0
Ukraine	-2.0	-2.0	-1.9	-1.8	-1.4	-1.0
Cluster East	**0.6**	**0.2**	**-0.2**	**-0.4**	**-0.6**	**-1.0**
Total	**1.2**	**1.1**	**0.9**	**0.9**	**0.9**	**0.8**

Table A13. Uniformity scenario: net population growth per thousand
of the total population

	1996	2000	2005	2010	2025	2050
Denmark	4.4	4.5	4.4	3.9	5.0	1.8
Finland	3.1	2.8	3.0	3.5	3.9	1.8
Iceland	6.9	6.1	5.9	6.4	7.7	2.6
Norway	5.7	5.3	4.6	4.5	6.2	1.8
Sweden	1.1	0.8	0.9	1.7	3.9	1.6
Cluster North	**3.2**	**2.9**	**2.9**	**3.2**	**4.7**	**1.7**
Austria	1.9	0.9	0.8	1.3	3.4	-0.4
Belgium	1.8	1.6	1.6	2.1	3.7	0.8
France	4.3	4.3	4.2	4.3	4.8	1.7
Germany	1.7	2.1	1.8	2.1	2.2	-0.1
Ireland	6.3	7.1	8.1	9.2	7.2	3.8
Luxembourg	12.9	10.4	8.1	6.9	6.0	2.0
Netherlands	5.3	5.5	4.6	4.3	4.9	0.9
Switzerland	3.7	2.5	1.7	2.1	3.4	-0.1
United Kingdom	3.6	3.2	3.2	3.8	5.3	2.0
Cluster West	**3.1**	**3.1**	**2.9**	**3.3**	**4.0**	**1.0**
Greece	1.8	2.5	2.8	2.4	1.1	-0.6
Italy	1.4	1.7	1.5	0.8	0.4	-1.8
Portugal	1.3	2.5	2.9	2.7	2.7	0.4
Spain	1.3	1.9	2.6	2.3	1.2	-1.6
Cluster South	**1.4**	**1.9**	**2.1**	**1.6**	**1.0**	**-1.4**
Croatia	-1.9	-1.1	-1.0	-1.0	-2.7	-1.3
Czech Republic	-1.2	-1.0	-1.7	-1.7	-2.5	-2.1
Estonia	-9.0	-5.6	-3.1	-1.9	-2.9	-0.7
Hungary	-3.6	-2.7	-2.3	-2.1	-1.5	-0.1
Latvia	-11.1	-7.0	-4.0	-2.5	-3.0	-2.1
Lithuania	-1.3	-1.2	-0.9	-0.6	-1.1	-1.1
Poland	0.9	0.5	1.2	1.7	0.3	0.0
Slovak Republic	1.6	2.0	2.2	1.9	0.2	-0.2
Slovenia	0.9	0.3	-0.4	-0.7	-2.5	-3.0
Cluster Central	**-0.7**	**-0.5**	**-0.1**	**0.3**	**-0.7**	**-0.5**
Belarus	-3.9	-2.7	-1.3	-0.9	-3.0	-1.7
Bulgaria	-4.6	-5.2	-5.0	-5.0	-5.0	-2.9
Moldavia	-3.2	-1.7	0.5	1.8	0.5	1.1
Romania	-4.3	-2.3	-0.7	0.0	-0.7	0.2
Russia	-3.9	-2.1	-0.6	-0.4	-2.8	-1.6
Ukraine	-10.5	-8.2	-5.8	-4.6	-3.7	-2.0
Cluster East	**-5.3**	**-3.5**	**-1.8**	**-1.3**	**-2.8**	**-1.5**
Total	**-0.5**	**0.3**	**0.9**	**1.2**	**0.9**	**-0.3**

Table A14. Diversity scenario: net population growth per thousand
of the population

	1996	2000	2005	2010	2025	2050
Denmark	4.4	3.5	2.6	1.6	1.1	-3.0
Finland	3.1	2.0	1.2	0.8	-1.1	-3.5
Iceland	6.9	4.8	3.2	2.4	1.2	-3.2
Norway	5.7	4.2	2.7	1.9	1.7	-3.1
Sweden	1.1	0.0	-0.7	-1.0	-1.1	-3.8
Cluster North	**3.2**	**2.1**	**1.1**	**0.6**	**0.0**	**-3.4**
Austria	1.9	0.4	-0.9	-1.5	-2.3	-7.4
Belgium	1.8	0.9	-0.1	-0.8	-1.9	-5.9
France	4.3	3.5	2.2	1.2	-0.8	-4.9
Germany	1.7	1.4	0.2	-0.3	-2.3	-6.5
Ireland	6.3	6.1	6.1	5.8	1.7	-2.2
Luxembourg	12.9	9.6	6.4	4.2	0.9	-4.4
Netherlands	5.3	4.8	2.9	1.7	-0.2	-5.6
Switzerland	3.7	1.9	0.2	-0.6	-2.3	-7.0
United Kingdom	3.6	2.6	1.8	1.5	0.3	-4.2
Cluster West	**3.1**	**2.4**	**1.3**	**0.7**	**-1.0**	**-5.4**
Greece	1.8	1.6	0.7	-0.5	-3.1	-7.3
Italy	1.4	0.7	-0.4	-1.8	-3.9	-8.8
Portugal	1.3	1.8	1.0	-0.2	-2.0	-6.1
Spain	1.3	1.0	0.4	-0.8	-3.3	-8.6
Cluster South	**1.4**	**1.0**	**0.1**	**-1.2**	**-3.5**	**-8.3**
Croatia	-2.2	-3.1	-4.6	-6.0	-9.6	-14.5
Czech Republic	-1.2	-1.1	-2.0	-3.0	-7.2	-13.7
Estonia	-9.0	-7.8	-6.9	-6.6	-10.3	-14.3
Hungary	-3.7	-3.1	-3.5	-4.5	-7.2	-11.9
Latvia	-11.1	-9.4	-7.9	-7.1	-10.4	-15.9
Lithuania	-1.3	-1.9	-2.1	-2.4	-6.2	-12.5
Poland	0.9	0.1	0.3	-0.1	-5.2	-11.9
Slovak Republic	1.5	1.4	1.1	0.1	-4.8	-11.9
Slovenia	0.8	0.1	-0.7	-2.2	-7.3	-14.7
Cluster Central	**-0.8**	**-1.1**	**-1.2**	**-1.8**	**-6.2**	**-12.5**
Belarus	-3.9	-3.9	-3.2	-3.6	-8.5	-17.5
Bulgaria	-4.9	-6.7	-7.5	-8.5	-12.4	-20.6
Moldavia	-3.2	-3.1	-2.4	-2.6	-8.0	-16.2
Romania	-4.3	-4.1	-4.4	-5.4	-9.4	-19.0
Russia	-4.0	-4.2	-4.1	-4.7	-9.3	-17.6
Ukraine	-10.5	-9.1	-8.1	-8.2	-10.9	-18.8
Cluster East	**-5.4**	**-5.2**	**-5.0**	**-5.5**	**-9.6**	**-18.0**
Total	**-0.5**	**-0.8**	**-1.3**	**-2.0**	**-4.6**	**-9.9**

Appendix 2

The Scenario Browser   ——

Corina HUISMAN and Evert VAN IMHOFF

1 | System requirements

The results of the scenarios may be inspected more in detail using the *Scenario Browser*: a program on CD-ROM that is included with this volume. The *Scenario Browser* was programmed in Delphi 3.0. It is an easy-to-use program that guides the user in making tables and charts of the scenario results. System requirements are a PC with a 386 or higher processor, a CD-ROM player and Windows 95 installed. The program will run from CD-ROM, or alternatively, for faster performance, it may be copied to the hard disk. Be sure to remove the auto-run program from the directory after copying the program and the data-subdirectory to the hard disk.

2 | Using the program

The program will start automatically after the CD-ROM is inserted in the CD-ROM player. In the opening screen a choice may be made between the required **Output types** of the results. Moreover, the **Clusters** button brings you to a map with more information about each cluster and individual countries within each cluster. By clicking on each individual country in the list for a chosen cluster a table appears with the base year demographic parameters of that country: base year population, TFR, E0 and net migration per 1000. By clicking on the **Assumptions** button in this screen the parameters of both scenarios pertaining to the chosen cluster appear. By clicking on the **Close** button the program returns to the opening screen.

In the opening screen menu there are five output types available:

1. Population tables
2. Events per year tables
3. Population pyramids
4. Population time series graphs
5. Events time series graphs

After selecting the output type, a second screen is opened and the user is requested to specify the dimensions of the table or the chart. The following dimensions are available:

Population tables:

1. Scenario: Uniformity/Diversity
2. Country (33; clusters)
3. Year (1996-2051)
4. Sex: M/V/T
5. Age: (0-99+; age groups)

Events per year:

1. Scenario: Uniformity/Diversity
2. Country (33)
3. Year (1996-2050)
4. Sex: M/V/T
5. Type of event: Net Migration, Births, Deaths, Life Expectancy, Total Fertility Rate, Net Migration per 1000

The output when choosing the Type of event is the quantitative specification of the scenario assumptions. They are not output results, but input parameters of the scenarios.

Population pyramids:

1. Scenario: Uniformity/Diversity
2. Country (33; clusters)
3. Year (1996-2051)

Sex and Age are included in the pyramids by definition. In addition, the user can choose between a number of chart options. More than one pyramid may be drawn in the same chart.

Population time series graphs:

1. Scenario: Uniformity/Diversity
2. Country (33; clusters)
3. Sex: M/V/T
4. Age: (0-99+; age groups)

Year is included in these graphs by definition. In addition, the user can choose between a number of chart options. More than one line may be drawn in the same chart.

Event time series graphs:

1. Scenario: Uniformity/Diversity
2. Country (33)
3. Sex: M/V/T
4. Type of event: Net Migration, Births, Deaths, Life Expectancy, Total Fertility Rate, Net Migration per 1000

Year is included in these graphs by definition. In addition, the user can choose between a number of chart options. More than one line may be drawn in the same graph.

After selecting the table dimensions, a third screen is opened with the specification of the required output format of the table. When more than two dimensions are selected, more than one table is necessary. The layout of this table can be controlled by the user.

3 | Exporting output to other programs

The results of the program may be exported to the clipboard, by selecting and copying the table or the graph. Note that the graph is exported as a bitmap, and cannot be changed after copying. The tables may be selected and copied to the clipboard. They should be pasted into a worksheet.